T0195932

Writing the Light

Finding the Light in the Darkness of Depression.
The Awakening of a Lightworker

PHOENIX ROSE

BALBOA.PRESS

A DIVISION OF HAY HOUSE

Balboa Press books may be ordered through booksellers or by contacting:

Balboa Press
A Division of Hay House
1663 Liberty Drive
Bloomington, IN 47403
www.balboapress.com
1 (877) 407-4847

Because of the dynamic nature of the Internet, any web addresses or
links contained in this book may have changed since publication and
may no longer be valid. The views expressed in this work are solely those
of the author and do not necessarily reflect the views of the publisher,
and the publisher hereby disclaims any responsibility for them.

The author of this book does not dispense medical advice or prescribe the use
of any technique as a form of treatment for physical, emotional, or medical
problems without the advice of a physician, either directly or indirectly. The
intent of the author is only to offer information of a general nature to help
you in your quest for emotional and spiritual well-being. In the event you use
any of the information in this book for yourself, which is your constitutional
right, the author and the publisher assume no responsibility for your actions.

If you would like to contact the author, you may reach
her at: authorphoenixrose@yahoo.com

Print information available on the last page.

ISBN: 978-1-9822-4186-5 (sc)
ISBN: 978-1-9822-3608-3 (e)

Balboa Press rev. date: 04/28/2020

There I was, lying under a car on the cold ground, in my pajamas, escaping a beaten from the husband I had been forced to marry at age seventeen. *How did I get to this point?* That's a bit of a lengthy but captivating story, which I will unravel, along with the even more tumultuous years that followed. The story itself is one in its own, but it is also the remarkable lessons learned that helped me overcome depression that arose from it. It is a story within a story—and both are extraordinary.

Foreword

"This is a story of resilience, the most valuable of human qualities, the one which allows a person to be knocked down by life and come back at least as strong as before. May the readers of this story be inspired to overcome any obstacles they may face".

- Dr. V, Psychiatrist from Bayshore, New York

Contents

> I'm a little pencil in the hand of a writing God, who is sending a love letter to the world.
>
> Mother Teresa

I rather write than read. I rather write than speak. If you want to have a deep conversation with me, send me an email. I've always been a better writer than speaker. I guess it's my heart that has something to say, not the mouth.

As a child until adulthood I would sit in solitude and write letters to myself, most times destroying them in fear that someone would read my private thoughts. I shared no secrets. They were conversations only to me, never to be found or exposed. Today, after years of battling and bottling tumultuous feelings inside, choking and desperately needing to breathe, writing became my air.

I have always been very private and hid my pain from the world. I maintained a character that withstood all obstacles and if I was suffering, it was unseen by the public. I had believed that the display of any kind of suffering was a sign of weakness. When I faced the world, I showed strength and an infallible character.

Today, I see courage where I once thought was weakness. I've come to understand that the more cracks, the stronger the character and that our past powerfully affects our present, as our present powerfully affects our future.

Mission

I am at a point in my life that I believe I am *not* to take all of these life's struggles to my grave. They happened for a reason. *You are my reason.* Through my suffering someone can heal. In order to do this, I have realized and accepted that I must completely surrender myself and open my heart to the reader by being brave, raw, honest, and open to judgment as I had never been able to be in the past; not even with my family or closest friends. So, I now willingly open my scars as I take this catharsis journey into various periods of my life, in the hopes that my pain will lead to someone's Healing. It is time to stand strong. It is time to reveal in order to heal; my healing as well as yours. This has become my life's purpose. You, the reader, are my purpose. THANK YOU.

Prologue

I am first generation American-born Eastern European, raised with the strict cultural upbringing of another land. Molded to be a virgin teenage bride destined for an arranged marriage, later married off in New York City to my stranger husband. A young girl lost in a big city trying to find my identity and later fighting for the freedom to be me. Surviving completely alone, I've encountered numerous heart-wrenching trials and failures, felt the torments of tragedies, betrayal, broken relationships, with a lack of love and bouts of extreme loneliness, I fell into a deep and dark state of depression lasting several years until finally surrendering to it and desiring death more than life.

On the brink of this suicidal state, through detailed events in this book, I was spiritually awakened and hope was restored hence this book was born with a purpose of saving not only myself, but to also provide healing to others.

Refusing to surrender to the darkness of depression, I have instead chose to begin **Writing the Light.**

Chapter 1
The Making of Me

If, when we are born, we could be who we are instead of what is expected of us (either by our parents, culture, or society), magic could happen. We would be able to unleash a power from within that could change the world. Unfortunately, and without blame, many people don't realize this soon enough, so like many, I was molded instead.

This landed me on the brink of suicide and delayed my life's purpose for decades.

I am the fifth-born of six children to non-fluent, Eastern European immigrant parents. I was born and raised in the Midwest in a loving home—but with the same strict, cultural upbringing and ethnic codes that our parents were raised by in their native land. It was obvious to me at a young age that we were very different than the other kids I went to school with. There was a clear culture clash as it was the complete opposite to an American lifestyle that exuded freedom and an open mind.

This strict upbringing was very beneficial to my character as it bred a lot of great traits such as respect, loyalty, and family values; many which, unfortunately, seem rare today. However, since I was extremely sheltered and protected from outside influences, it also caused major setbacks in my maturity and growth as an individual. Even as an adult, I was still very naive, close-minded, innocent, and overly trusting of the world. I had to learn things that most already knew by high school if not sooner. I had to learn through ridicule, painful mistakes, being taken advantage of, and swift kicks in the ass.

I had been molded into what a young woman was expected to be instead of who I was. In our culture, for instance, the girls were strictly raised to become housewives and mothers by an arranged marriage by their late teens. This was all I knew, and it seemed normal to me. This molding was so deeply instilled in me that it took me many, many years to figure out who I was, what I wanted, and to learn to live my life for myself and not for what was expected by my culture and family. For years, I was lost and had no sense of identity.

My story is the consequence of the reality of circumstance that led to an interesting yet many times excruciating road to personal growth and life. This road to my life's journey was a movie that would have one cry many times over, as I have, as I had to relive it to share it with you.

Early On

As a child, I was very loving and playful, and I enjoyed writing and singing. I was mature, very self-disciplined, and obedient, and I always excelled in school. My dad always said that out of all six of his kids, I was the child who he never had to put much effort in disciplining.

I lost my mother in an accident when I was ten, so my father was everything to me. I saw him as a godlike figure. He was very strict, but I've always felt safe and protected by him. I worshipped his ideas, opinions, and thoughts and made them my own. He also had a way of making you think through his head and not your own (as many parents do), so in my youth, I had almost no opinions that weren't his.

He barely spoke English, but he was very wise and had great money-management skills. Although we had a large family, we always had a better home and furnishings than other people on our block. I felt proud of him. Still do. Today, he has become one of my best friends, and he has been very understanding and supportive through my struggles.

Growing up, we weren't allowed to hang out with kids from other cultures outside of school to avoid being influenced against our cultural upbringing, traditions, and beliefs. We had to be proud, respectful, and devoted to our nationality and maintaining it.

My father was protective of all his children, but he was especially strict with his daughters. I never slept over at anyone's home. If I needed to go to the corner store, I would have to take one of my brothers with me. I was not allowed to join any extracurricular activities that would require me staying afterschool—I *really* wanted to play basketball—and when I was in the third grade, I couldn't even go on an overnight camping trip with my class. I never got over that one and still have never been camping.

As a teenager, it was obvious that I was very naive compared to the other girls my age. By high school, many of my classmates were having sexual relationships, smoking, cursing, and hanging out late, none of which was tolerated or even spoke of in our home, because we knew when something was not allowed and didn't have to be told.

I didn't understand half of the things that the girls at school would talk about. I remember one day in the eleventh grade when one of my school friends asked me, "Do you like to be on top?" She must have assumed that I was sexually active. I was brought up very sheltered and had absolutely no clue what that meant. I thought, *On top of what?* I imagine my puzzled look stopped her from waiting for a reply. I was beyond naïve when it came to those things, but I did surpass most of my classmates academically and was on the National Honor Society.

My life consisted of only home and school, but I was very happy since I had a big, loving family to share it with. I knew nothing else. This was my norm.

I was not allowed to wear makeup or shorts once I became a teenager, or play with boys other than my brothers. Dating was forbidden since arranged marriages were practiced in our culture. Today, arranged marriages are still practiced in many countries and in many different religious backgrounds.

I was raised strictly to become a good wife and mother. By the age of sixteen, I already knew how to make homemade bread from scratch and woke up early on weekends to knead it and have it ready for breakfast. I did, in fact, feel the importance of learning how to cook, clean, and maintain a home, but getting an education always felt most important to me. Luckily, my father also stressed this importance unlike some of the more close-minded village types that took their daughters out of school at an early age so they could just marry and become housewives. I was raised to be a whole woman who could bring home the bacon *and* fry it up in a pan.

In our ethnic code of laws, if a bride was not a virgin, she would be returned to her parents—and the family would be disgraced by the community. This was a big deal. It was a very proud culture, and morality was king. Therefore, it was mandatory that I was to remain pure, with my virginity intact, until marriage.

There was a tactic used in our home to keep track of my periods, which I didn't realize until years later. My stepmom stored the sanitary napkins in our parents' bedroom where no one was ever allowed, so when I needed them each month, I would have to go through her to get them, assuring that I got my monthly cycle— hence, not pregnant. At that time, I just thought that's where they were kept. I was too innocent to think any other way. Hell, I was so innocent that I used to get embarrassed if someone were kissing on television (remember the Big Red commercial where you can kiss a little longer?) and would look away or down at my feet. However, I guess they had to guarantee and take the precautions they felt necessary to avoid any chance of the family being humiliated and disgraced.

I was raised to believe in the ethics of an arranged marriage and knew it would happen to me at some point. All my friends of the same cultural background who I grew up with were getting arranged marriages, and their parents and my parents were products of arranged marriages, so it seemed normal to me. My sister had been arranged to marry a handsome young man, and they were a very attractive couple who seemed happy at the time. When my time came, I expected it to be a fairytale union also—just as any fantasy-driven teenage girl would. I pictured marrying some nice, cute boy and living happily ever after.

Unfortunately, my fantasy turned out to be a nightmare instead.

Chapter 2
Little Girl, Big City

A s culture had it, at the ripe age of seventeen, I was engaged. Ripe meant virginity intact, but for me, ripe didn't mean ready. Although I expected to marry young, I was still shocked when I was actually engaged. I did not feel ready to have sexual relations or be someone's wife. I didn't have any desire to be a mother yet since I still felt like a child myself. My only desire and focus at that time was to finish school. It was my education that made me feel like I would become a woman—not becoming someone's wife.

However, I was not allowed to decide when and who I was to marry. It was decided for me. Arranged marriages usually occur when a girl is in her teens to a man approved by her father. I was brought up to obey my father and my culture, and I was not allowed to voice rejection or to assume I knew better. So, now engaged, I would soon be sent from where I was raised in a small city in the Midwest to my husband, a complete stranger, in New York City.

I couldn't imagine being married even before finishing high school or living in New York City, which seemed like a huge, scary place where I knew no one and would live incredibly far away from my family. I would be a scared, little closed-minded virgin lost in a big city full of strangers.

When I finally met the man that I was engaged to, I was very disappointed. He was much older than I was, and I was not attracted to him in the least bit. I was so very sad and secretly crying during my four-month engagement. "Secretly" because it was considered shameful to disapprove of the man who was chosen for you, or to go against the family and culture. Reality struck hard when I officially became engaged. Before that, I had no problems with my culture and respected its traditions, but now I felt like a piece of meat being sold at an auction. However, since I was raised to believe that this was my destiny, I believed I had no choice but to accept my fate and live it.

I felt like my life was over before it had even begun.

Four months later, I boarded a plane with bridesmaids and men, leaving my hometown and everyone that I knew, and was sent to my wedding that same evening in New York City where I knew absolutely no one—not even my husband!

I must mention that I was in my wedding dress at the airport and during the flight. I felt ridiculous as I walked past the terminals in it, looking pathetic and sad. It was my first time walking in heels, and it hurt like hell as I waddled through the airport. It was also my first time ever having makeup on. I had never had my eyebrows plucked—including on that day. Thanks for that! The only cool part was going on a plane for the first time.

As I walked through the airport in my wedding dress, people began to clap until I got nearer, and they saw my miserably unhappy face at which point there were moments of silence and confusion. Finally, a woman asked my sister, "Why does she look so sad?" It was not that I had anything to be happy about, but even so, I couldn't smile since it was considered shameful to appear happy. You were leaving your family and going to sleep with a man for the first time. You should have shame and be embarrassed. That was the mentality. Imagine that. Marriage should be a celebration—not a mourning.

The man I married was a man who spoke little English and whose ego was even larger than his receding hairline. He lacked an educational background. I could not imagine having to spend my life with him, let alone have him be my first kiss. It was repulsive.

Our first conversation occurred as I lay shaking in his bed on our wedding night. I had zero desire to give my virginity up to someone I did not know or love. I was not even attracted to him. I did not, and literally could not, have sex with him. I felt so hopeless and wore a sanitary napkin on my wedding night and for several days to follow in the hope that it would keep him away from me and help save my virginity for as long as I could. It was a desperate attempt that wouldn't last long before he realized what I was doing.

Shortly after, he complained, and I began to cry, plead, and beg that I wasn't ready to have sex and to please not force me to do it. This became an argument every single night for two months. Each night, I fell asleep exhausted and dreaded waking up every morning having to face another day of fighting for my dignity. It was emotionally exhausting.

Custom had it that you return to visit your family in the three weeks after marriage as a woman—no longer a virgin. Well, little did they know that when I returned, I was *still* a virgin. My husband was furious and felt emasculated, but because of it, he didn't tell on me. Traditionally, I was not to refuse anything my husband asked of me that a wife should provide, yet I put up a fight every single night and refused to give up my virginity. I told him that I had agreed to be his wife and would do anything he expected of me but please not that. If my family knew that I hadn't consummated my marriage, they would have been enraged since it was a shameful act of disobedience to my husband.

He kept threatening that he was going to return me to my family. I was mortified of the embarrassment and shame that I would cause my family or even the mention of my name associated to anything sex related. I began to hysterically cry and continued to beg that he please wait until I felt ready.

He was furious and yelled, "What the hell did I get married for?"

I felt like a worthless piece of meat sold like cattle. I had accepted to be his wife—not that I could not accept—but I did not want to give up the only thing that was pure and sacred to me. There would be nothing left of me. I would be nothing. No dignity. I started seeing my cultural codes as unacceptable. I could not accept that someone else could decide that I was ready and decide to whom. It sickened and saddened me greatly. I believe it was the first experience I had where my true self and my own personal beliefs surfaced instead of those that were instilled in me.

Every step of my life was controlled since birth. I felt like I had no voice and no rights. *If this is going to be my life, what am I supposed to look forward to?*

After two months of fighting—exhausted and feeling completely defeated with no one to defend or protect me—I gave in. I was repulsed and disgusted, and tears streamed down my face as I gave my body to a man I had no desire or feelings for.

I felt like a prostitute.

Afterward, I remember crying in my shower and feeling as though the water would never be able to wash away my feelings of filth, sin, and shame. I felt like a victim of a crime that I had not committed.

A piece of paper made him my husband, but in reality, he was a stranger who had just raped me.

I hated myself and secretly resented my family and my culture for years to follow. Feelings of abandonment followed, and I still struggle with them today. The feelings of comfort, security, and love that I felt in my family growing up were replaced by fear, worthlessness, and despair. My nightmare had just begun.

****

Our code of ethics taught that you got married once, and that chosen man would be your only man as long as you live. Getting divorced is like making the entire family wear a scarlet letter, being ridiculed, tainted, and the gossip of the town. The divorced woman would be considered used, unwanted, damaged goods, and/or of low morale for not being submissive and tolerant. I knew that if I got out of that marriage, I would be considered the reason the family was constantly looked down upon. It was a heavy weight on the shoulders of a teenager who loved her family immensely.

As the years went by, I was never happy in my so-called marriage. It was clear that he married me to be his maid and sex slave. I cooked, cleaned, and obeyed as I was molded to do. He never tried to do anything to please me.

As if the absence of kindness wasn't enough, he was a heavy gambler and was physically abusive. He frequently came home angry after several hours, sometimes days, of heavy gambling and losing money at the bar he owned, and he would release his anger on me through physical abuse. I recall one particular beating when he blamed me and said that he had to spend thousands to marry me. I would've spent thousands not to have to.

For some years, I firmly believed that I had no other choice but to live and die with him since divorce was too heavy a price to pay for my family and my reputation in a community that was extremely judgmental and unforgiving. I kept thinking of the great shame that I would cause my family if I were to get divorced more than I cared about my own happiness. So, I endured, sacrificing my own happiness for theirs and feeling like it was a small price to pay. My husband took advantage of this, knowing that I would rather endure the pain of his abuse than hurt my father or my family.

I was a daddy's girl, and I did not want to disappoint him. I wanted to make him proud, and in his presence, I pretended everything was fine. I never told anyone in my family how miserable I was. Since I didn't think it would do any good, I held it inside for years. I only fronted a smile when I was in their presence on my visits back home to see them. I became quite talented at pretending or saving face. The only time I felt any kind of genuine happiness was when I was around my relatives. I became a kid again.

During the first months of marriage, I was a senior in high school. One morning, like many others, I asked if he would give me some money for lunch since he was my only source of income. He threw it at me and said that I had to have sex with him to keep it. He tried this more than once. I would have rather starved.

What kind of a human being was he? A pig of a man.

If my family ever knew this, even today, they would rightfully give him the punishment that he deserves, but I never told a soul. It was so incredibly humiliating. Feelings of worthlessness started to overcome me.

Luckily for me, he only came home a few days a week since he did a lot of all-nighters at the gambling clubs he hung out at. The less I had to see his face, the more enduring my life was.

Every time he lost bets and drank, he would come home angry. One night, he came home sometime after midnight, as usual, and found me sleeping. He tried to smother me with a pillow in my sleep. I began experiencing anxiety and lived in constant fear for my life. I began sleeping with a knife under my mattress. I figured I would kill him before he killed me. Not that I cared about the value of my life during those years, but he did not deserve to take it.

Prior to that arrangement, I was a very happy, loving, sweet, peacefully natured, shy, and respectful girl. However, this abusive lifestyle definitely began to harden me and strengthen—or maybe crack—my character. Through the years of my misery, abuse, and having to submit sexually against my wishes to this peasant man, I had become the complete opposite of who I once was. I grew to be angry, cold, bitter, and damaged in many ways. I even became immune to the pain of his punches, having felt them so many times, expecting and receiving them at any given moment. Being with him hurt more than the physical pain he inflicted upon me. I was miserable.

There were many times I couldn't leave the house for several days at a time due to my bruises. I started to hate myself every time I looked in the mirror. I hated how I allowed myself to be treated. I felt unloved and abandoned by everyone. I thought, *What did I do to deserve this life? I was such a good daughter, sister, and student?*

I still cry when these feelings resurface and the scars reopen. I guess you never heal from certain painful experiences.

The best parts of me were dying each year I stayed with him. I felt like a withering flower. He took the sun out of my life. Still only a teenager, I constantly felt like I was paying a life sentence for something I never did.

About two years into the marriage, a friend of my father who lived in New York City noticed bruises on my face as I walked past him on the street. Unbeknownst to me, concerned, he called my father and told him. Shortly after, my father and my three brothers made a surprise visit and drove to New York to have a *talk* with my husband to warn him that I was not to be mistreated!

By our code of ethics, as long as your wife doesn't lie, cheat, or steal, she is to be taken care of and treated respectfully.

My father spoke to me in private and told me that he didn't marry me off to get abused, that I should tell him if this was happening, and that he shouldn't find out from others. This meant a lot to me, and I respected and loved my father and brothers for coming to my rescue. They did love me. They did want to protect me.

I desperately wanted out of this miserable existence of a marriage, but divorce was considered shameful and would cause turmoil for the family and my reputation. I thought, *I will only be arranged again to someone else—possibly to someone even worse. Just stay in it and shut up.* I did not own my life at that time and never thought I could.

After my family delivered their warning to my husband, it seemed to soften him. I felt safer, but it was an act that he displayed while they were there. He waited until they left to drive back, and then he gave me a beating. He told me if they ever found out again, he would destroy me.

Later, he delivered his beatings to my body and avoided my face. I remember after one such beating having purple and blue bruises all over my shoulders.

At that point, I knew that if my family were to find out that he continued mistreating me for no just cause and disrespected their warning, the code, and did not hold his word to my father, they will demolish him. I didn't want my father or brothers to go to jail because of me. They meant the world to me. I would rather endure his physical abuse myself than live with the pain and/or problems that I would be causing them. My life didn't matter as much as they mattered to me, and that was the bottom line. My loyalty was unwavering.

My husband knew this and used it to his advantage.

***

As the years went by, I started to grow balls (yes, I just said that). One night when my husband (ugh, I hate calling him that) called me in the middle of the night to pick him up from the club he gambled at, as he usually did, he got a surprise response.

He never cared that I had to work in the morning (to try to pay bills as he gambled his checks away). Well, this night, when I was awakened by his call, my courage was also awakened and finally, I responded "No! Take a cab!"

I was brought up strict, and we never ever talked back to the man of the house, so this was a first.

He could not believe his ears, and at first, he was silent, but then he said, "If you don't come right now, I will come home and beat the leaving hell out of you and burn your car!"

I had bought the car at an auction. It was the only thing that was mine.

His threat didn't scare me since he often abused me, but I thought it would be worse than other times since this time it was actually my fault (for talking back). So, I prepared for his arrival and put extra blankets on the bed to protect me from the beating I was about to receive. For the first time, I felt like it would be worth it.

Minutes later, I heard the key in the door, and my heart started racing. He came straight to the bedroom, and the abuse started. However, this time, something different happened. As I tried to hide myself under the blankets, as protection from his punches, I felt something inside of me began to roar. Out of nowhere, I threw the covers over me and punched him dead in his face!

I immediately ran out of the house to escape him.

I didn't know where I was going, but I kept running barefoot and frightened for several blocks into the night. I looked back and saw him running after me. Finally, I ran into someone's yard and crawled under a parked car.

A few seconds later, I saw his feet slowly passing by. He was searching for me. Facedown in the cold dirt, in my pajamas, I felt my heart beating out of my chest. Thankfully, he didn't find me. I watched him slowly walk in another direction.

I stayed under that car, barefoot, on that cold ground in the middle of the night, for what felt like hours. I was shaking and shivering. I thought, *What will I do now? Where will I go?* I was afraid to return home. I was afraid to go back to my family in the Midwest after this shame I had just caused them by dishonoring my husband. If I went back, I knew I would only end up in another arranged marriage.

I was twenty-one years old, a bright and innocent girl from a good family, barefoot, in pajamas, lying facedown under a parked car in the cold dirt. I couldn't even cry. I couldn't even blink. I was numb to the life I had been given. I didn't deserve that. I felt so ashamed. I was ashamed of myself for allowing my life to get to that point. I felt so extremely alone. Miles away from my family. I felt like I had no home—nowhere.

I am in a bookstore as I write this, and tears are streaming down my face as I relive this time. The people sitting around me are looking at me, and a couple are whispering to each other, but I just can't stop the tears from falling. I have my earphones in (as usual). I like to listen to nature music sounds for therapeutic purposes while I write, but even that's not helping. Although this event happened more than twenty years ago, it makes my chest burn in pain to think of how young and innocent I was to have lived such a sad life so young. At this point in my life, I could have a daughter that age, and it would break my heart.

I wish I had my mother.

***

With nowhere else to go, I eventually returned to the apartment I shared with him after I made sure he wasn't there. When he returned the next night, I pretended to be asleep, but I kept one eye open, fearing my safety. Surprisingly, he left me alone but I didn't trust him.

A few days later, as I was driving my car near the George Washington Bridge, I heard a large thump. Suddenly, the car started to slow down, and then it eventually stopped completely before reaching the toll booths. Perplexed, I leaned forward and looked at the hood, which appeared to be melting. It was! My friend and I got out and started running away from it, thinking it would explode and kill both of us. Within seconds, a large flame shot straight up out from the engine. It was several feet high.

Shortly after, the Port Authority came and used some purple spray to stop the fire. My used car, my only real possession, was melted. I asked the men who towed it if they could tell what caused it, and they told me it most likely was electrical. I couldn't help but wonder if my husband wired it since he specifically said he was going to burn it just a few days before when I refused to pick him up.

I could have died. Is he trying to kill me? Will he succeed next time?

After four years and three months, I had reached my breaking point. I finally called my father and told him I couldn't do it anymore. He was beyond words and I knew my decision made him look at me disgracefully at that time. The entire family would pay the price of my decision.

The next day, I went to the courthouse and got an order of protection. I arranged to have police officers escort him out of our apartment and out of my life. I left his belongings in garbage bags on the curb.

Garbage to garbage.

***

Everything about me changed during that miserable existence: my personality, my character, and my belief system. I was forced to grow up very quickly. Due to my circumstances, I became bitter and cold. However, I also became fearless, independent, and strong. I came to a point where I would rather die than continue to live as someone's slave and be a prisoner in my own life. I could not continue to care about what others thought of me if I were to get divorced.

My loyalty for my family was there and always would be, but I couldn't be expected to live that way.

I was full of anger and rebellious, and thought, *The hell to anyone who doesn't support me and the happiness and freedom I desire and deserve! My happiness should matter more than the opinions of others. Fuck the scarlet letter! The hell to everyone! I don't need anyone!*

I couldn't take another minute of that life. *Forgive me, that after four years and three months of being physically and emotionally abused, and forced to have sex with someone I was repulsed by, did not work!*

I thought it was insane to be judged in a negative light for having endured everything I had gone through. I could no longer accept *that* as normal. Arranged marriages were barbaric. Not for me. Not for my unborn children. I was pushed to my limits and rebelled. I knew that I had to take control of my own life, and I did. I became strong-willed, fearless, and determined. I was ready to lose everything for my freedom!

I *finally* realized that the opinions of others did not outweigh the price of my happiness in this short life. The cultural stigma was not going to own me. I was not going to be stripped of my own identity. My life had purpose, and I was determined to take that road. I would risk losing anyone who didn't support me. I was very angry and could not care any less than I felt cared for. Nothing on this planet should take precedence over my happiness, and anyone who loved me should love me unconditionally. Otherwise, I would rather be without them.

It was a monumental time in my life. I was finally evolving and becoming who I really was. I was ready to take charge of my own life—even if I was completely alone.

Chapter 3
Freedom with a Price

O ur code of laws also stated that if a divorce was to transpire, the divorced daughter was expected to move back into her parents' home. It was seen as shameful to be a free woman, living alone or dating. I would be arranged again to another stranger, but this time, since I was divorced and no longer a virgin, my choices would be slimmer. Most likely, I would be married off to a divorced man with children, a widower, or an undesirable man. After that experience, I was petrified and had zero desire to ever get married again. I could not risk repeating that ordeal. I wanted nothing more than my freedom to find myself and make my own life. I decided to go against my family and cultural code, and I refused to move back to the Midwest with my family.

This was devastating news to my father since he lived for his family name being respected and honored. Everyone in my family was in disbelief about my decision and that I would ever disrespect the code or my father. However, I didn't see it as disrespect. It was my only choice to have a chance of happiness.

Four years prior, the idea that I would ever do something like that would have been unimaginable to me or them. Our cultural community in America was very involved, judgmental, and controlling—unaware of how suffocating it could be for families and their children to maintain their cultural beliefs in a free country.

Even so, I could no longer live being judged for every step I made, having every mistake put under a sharp-lensed microscope, or constantly being told how I should be living my life versus how I wanted to live it. I knew that I would *never* be happy in a controlled environment. I wanted to learn from life. *Let me make my own mistakes. Let me fall, get back up, and feel the pains of life. Otherwise, how will I really learn or know what I want?*

When my oldest brother found out that I decided to stay in New York City, he said, "How can I protect you if you're so far?"

It warmed my heart. I didn't realize how my decision was going to affect each family member in different ways. All I could think about was how desperately I wanted to just be happy. For once, I was being selfish.

The choice to move back home to the Midwest with my family was always there. They were hopeful that I would return, but as much as I was in love with them, going back was never an option for me. I was no longer the girl that left that house just four years prior. I had been changed in so many ways and on so many levels. My freedom now meant everything to me. It was *that* important. Without it, my life had no meaning or purpose. I could not live unless I was the only one controlling my mind, future, and life. I was a true American.

***

After going through so much of what many don't go through in a lifetime, by the time I was twenty-one, I was finally free. I evolved *much* stronger and wiser and was ready to have a life with meaning. It had been more than four years since I had smiled from the heart. It was time.

My only desire was to live far away from anyone who knew me and that part of my life and start all over as if it had never happened. I didn't want to be looked down upon or judged for what I'd been through. I didn't want to be around those small-minded gossipers. *I know my worth. The hell to those who do not.*

Unfortunately, at first, I couldn't be happy. Although I had gained my freedom, I felt like I had to disgrace my family and my reputation in the process. Gossip about my running away from my husband had consumed my family. Choosing to live alone and remain in New York made it even worse. It made me look like I was the bad one in the marriage. However, I knew 1,000,000 percent that living alone and away from everyone was what I needed to do. In the process, I hurt those I loved the most. I felt guilty and sad about it every day. It weighed very heavy on my heart for some time.

Although living alone was my choice, I still struggled with feelings of abandonment. I walked through the streets to and from work, head down, with a heavy, dark cloud above me. I felt like I was living in a fog. I had my freedom, but I had hurt my family in the process. It was very important for me to know that they still loved me. Because of this, it took time for me to *allow* myself to be happy and to learn to let go and live for me.

For weeks, I struggled with the pain I had unintentionally inflicted upon my family, but at the same time, I felt such a great relief to never have to see or deal with my ex ever again—or so I thought.

One afternoon, after I locked up the medical office where I worked, I turned around and saw him across the street. He was leaning against a car and pointing a gun directly at me.

I froze, but I didn't feel any fear at all. I thought, *I've had enough!* I didn't run or duck—or even think to do so. I already felt half dead inside because I didn't know if my family loved me anymore. I had nothing to lose. Without a second thought, I dropped my handbag, opened my arms wide like Jesus, and yelled, "Shoot, motherfucker!" I stood there and waited for a bullet like I was waiting for the bus.

Seconds later, he grunted and then pretended to laugh—as if to mask his failure at scaring me. He then slowly put the gun down, got in his car, and drove away.

I thought, *What a worthless piece of shit to do that to me, knowing that I had no family in New York to protect me. It wasn't enough that he took four years and three months of my precious life?*

Luckily, he never bothered me again. I was no longer that little girl who once tolerated it.

Note to Readers

It is very important that you understand that I have a very loving and supportive family. I carry no blame on them for any misfortune that has happened to me. They never even knew most of my hardships because I never told them. I endured it all alone to avoid creating trouble or being a burden.

The tradition of arranged marriages was instilled in our parents by their forefathers. It was how they lived for centuries. In today's society, sometimes they work—and sometimes they just don't. We all grew together, through these experiences and hardships, in a world of changing times, and we realize that we require change ourselves. Today, together as a strong, bonded, loving family, we support and love one another limitlessly.

Also, let it be very clear that I come from a culture that I am proud of. I do not mention the specific country my family is from because it has nothing to do with my misfortunes—and I do not wish the ignorance of undeserving subjection to it. So, in no way does my own personal experience mean that my culture as a whole should be poorly regarded. In reality, although many of the codes are now outdated, the culture itself is rich in beauty, history, family values, loyalty, honor, respect, and other notable traditions. It is a culture worthy of much praise.

As for arranged marriages, they are still practiced and considered normal in many countries today. Interestingly, I read that they have been proven to hold a significantly lower divorce rate than non-arranged marriages. Although it is not something I ever want to experience again, I know of dozens of people—and even many of my own relatives—who live or have lived beautiful, happy lives with their arranged significant others. Also worthy of mentioning are the kings and queens throughout Europe who wed this way to form alliances between countries for power, wealth, and other benefits.

Everyone has their own story. This just happens to be mine.

Starting Over and Moving On

As time went on, I became more and more independent. I did not feel alone or lonely at all. I imagined, in time, my family would get over my decision, and they have. Although they lived far, and I dearly missed them, I felt that I finally belonged to something. I belonged to myself. I never felt the feeling of freedom before, and it was clearly a feeling worth waking up to daily. I was finally happy and felt so hopeful. I was using my own mind and thoughts and making my own decisions. It was very liberating. My strict upbringing greatly helped guide my path with a strong sense of morality, self-discipline, and ethics.

As the years went by, I took control of my life. I began to heal and get to know who I was as an individual. I loved to work and was very responsible. I was also quite funny. I felt alive and happy. I smiled every day—many times a day. I loved music and singing. I liked me. I loved the new friends I made, and I was loyal to them. They became my only family in New York, and I cherished them.

I worked hard to support myself, never relying on anyone to pay my bills; many times, I tirelessly worked two jobs. I was determined not to fail or have to run back to my family for help. The cost of my freedom was priceless, and I was determined to succeed.

I enrolled in college and set out for a career in the medical field. I worked and went to college full-time, taking six trains per day and paying my own way through college. I loved this newfound freedom and the ability to take charge and direction of my life. I did it all seemingly effortlessly. I excelled quickly and became very independent. I relished in my freedom and individuality.

The past became a faint memory. It was as if I took a pill and forgot it all. I didn't want any association with that part of my past, and I would not allow it to stay a part of me. For years, I never told new friends or coworkers that I was ever (arranged) married. I buried it like the death that it was. I still have friends of over fifteen years who don't know about that part of my life. I didn't want any sympathy or attention brought to it. Mentally, I didn't even allow myself to revisit those memories. If a thought came to my mind, I immediately shot it out. I was mentally strong.

I was proud of the lady I was becoming, and I never wanted to allow anyone to make me feel inferior again. I worked very hard to put the self-worth back in me, where it belonged.

Unfortunately, years later, this desire to be alone, which I craved and sacrificed so much for, would later become my demon—as you will learn in later chapters.

Chapter 4
Moving Forward

A couple of years later, as I was moving forward with my life with happiness, confidence, and drive, I was sadly reminded that no matter how hard we try, sometimes we just can't escape our past—and we will always be "judged by sinners."

One day, an older female patient came into the doctor's office where I worked for an examination. She happened to be of the same cultural background as I was. Recognizing that I was of the same nationality, she started asking me the usual million nosy questions to find out who I was, who my parents were, my age, religion—blah-blah-blah—probably with the intention of getting me arranged with someone she knew, especially since I was considered attractive and had a good job.

When she asked if I was engaged or married, I confidently responded with my new modern mind-set and told her that I preferred to meet someone on my own.

She gasped in disgust and said, "No one wants a chicken after it laid an egg!"

Basically, she was telling me that no decent man would want a woman who wasn't a virgin or who was meeting men on her own (without family arranging it).

My modern mentality was not accepted or tolerated, but I no longer gave a rat's ass about their small-minded opinions. Truth be told, as ignorant as her remark was, it bothered me enough to add it to this book because in this culture I would always be judged or labeled for a divorce from a marriage I never wanted. At the time, it made me wonder if I would have to wear a scarlet letter for the rest of my life.

A main reason this bothered me so much was because, at that point in my life, I still only desired to be with a man of my own cultural background, but this time with someone like me: born here, hopefully more Americanized, with the ability to cultivate *both* cultures into something beautiful, more modern, and open-minded.

Where would I find one whose entire family was accepting of my divorced status? It was challenging, and this was a major setback in my relationships since I only dated from a small pool instead of the ocean of opportunity that the world offered in good men from any culture. But it was important to me to keep the family bond and tradition strong. I thought we would understand each other's families, lifestyle, upbringing, music, language, and traditions. I believed that it would make most sense and be the best choice. It was also important to me that my father could communicate with him since his English was limited. Maybe I also wanted to subconsciously heal the pain I had inflicted upon him.

Yet, this narrow-minded belief of only dating from this small pool of choices didn't allow for personal or worldly growth—and it didn't prove to be right for me. However, I was stuck in that trance for several years. I wouldn't even consider a single date with a man of any other culture. Doctor or lawyer, it did not matter—I declined them all. I thought, *If I wouldn't marry them, why bother dating them?* I was so businesslike in that area of my life, but it was bad business. It seems so insane now.

Seeking a Loving Partner

I was financially secure, supporting myself, and living alone. Although I felt free, and not lonely at all, I still wanted to be loved and know love. Unfortunately, at the time, I believed *anything* better than my previous and only relationship would be a good one. My lack of experience and being alone without guidance led me to find love in all the wrong places. I was still extremely naive and trusting, which led me to many painful heartaches and failed relationships instead.

In the mind of any sensible, logical, and intelligent person, this does not merit judgment or criticism. It merits compassion and understanding. I say this because those who have not evolved mentally and continue to live like the small-minded breed have often attempted to judge me for my mistakes and lack of experience. Years after my divorce, I was even shamelessly told that; I was called a whore because I had dated more than one man. Imagine the ignorance of the person who said that, believed it or had the stupidity and nerve to repeat it.

A whore? That is the most degrading insult for a person of my integrity especially since my character and morale were never in question in any of my relationships. Ironically, the only time I ever felt like a whore was when I was forced to repeatedly have sex with the stranger I was made to marry.

In reality, I was never a casual dater. I desired the stability found in a long-term relationship, and I wanted to enrich my life with more happiness and the feeling of belonging with a loving companion. Not everyone is fortunate enough to meet their perfect partner on the first date.

Love

Without it, do we really exist—or are we just taking up space?
Without it, are we truly happy?
How sad and painful it is to live life with an empty heart;
one that wants to be loved yet feels it is not.
Imagine life without it.
Imagine a heart without blood.

Imagine a flower without rain.
Imagine the day without the sun.
Imagine my face without a smile.

For most of my life, love was the piece of the puzzle that was not always there when everything else was. All the materialistic things of the world could be at my hands, and many were, but I would've traded them all in, in an instant, for love. It is the necessity in life that gives you the feeling that nothing else can. You cannot substitute it with a temporary feeling for that fades; true love never fades.

If it is all that everyone really needs, then why are some of us afraid of it? Do we not feel worthy of it? Or is it because love is pain—as I was once told and reminded? I would rather live with this pain than the emptiness of not knowing it—or, worse, never having it.

In Matters of the Heart

When I was about two years old, I was sitting in a kiddie pool in our backyard with a girl who was about a year older than I was.

The little girl defecated in the pool, and one of our moms noticed it floating and yelled, "Ugh! Who did that?"

The little girl quickly pointed at me.

Without skipping a beat, I slapped her across her face. Both mothers couldn't help but start laughing because they were very surprised at my behavior since I was normally a very sweet and well-behaved child. However, that one moment showed so much of what was in my personality even at such a young age. Even today, I still loathe dishonesty.

As an adult, I am still abhorrent to it. I would rather know the truth—even if it hurts—than be lied to. I don't want a sugar-coated answer to pacify me, and those who know me know that they will get an honest answer if they ask my opinion on something.

On top of being an honest person, I was raised very closed-minded, which made me very innocent and trusting of the world. I have crossed paths with people who took advantage of it most of my life—in friendships and in other relationships. It caused me a great deal of pain. It was a painful reality that people weren't as honest and kind as they should be.

In matters of the heart, specifically love, I've always suffered from a lack of it. Many times, I thought I had found it in places that it did not even exist. I believed in it and needed it, and I fought hard to make it work.

When I gave myself in a relationship, it was wholeheartedly. I would take care of that person just as I would myself, if not more. I was the perfect girlfriend, never needing a lot of attention and never asking for any material things. I just needed the respect and love I deserved, desired, and gave. That was everything to me. Morally, I was completely faithful, loyal, and sincere. All I desired was a man with similar qualities. I wasn't unrealistic in my desires, but I *was* fishing in a small pond of men.

I had a lot of failed relationships, which I will share in detail in the next chapter. Sometimes they were impossible relationships, yet I still accepted being in them, probably subconsciously believing that I was impossible myself. I tried and fought against all obstacles just to make it work, but no matter what, when it inevitably had to end, I was left feeling like a failure and in a great deal of pain because I knew that I had given it 100 percent.

Later, I found it much easier to break up a relationship myself if I saw signs of instability since the feelings of abandonment were just too heavy to endure. I am aware that this is a result of past pain, and I am no longer that person.

Chapter 5
Love and Relationships

I will now share certain relationship experiences that have had profound effects on me to show you who I was and how I finally broke.

I will refer to my exes not by their names but by their astrological signs. For those of you who study or enjoy astrology and its compatibility traits, I am a Capricorn. However, please understand that I do not intend to insult any particular sign by the character (or lack of) of any of these specific individuals. That would be senseless.

The Libra

He was my first boyfriend and the first time I ever fell in love. Those were the happiest years of my life to date!

His gentle and quiet nature captivated me. He was handsome, had dirty blond hair and green eyes, and was always neatly dressed. We lived in the same neighborhood. We would share a few seconds of eye contact every time we crossed paths, clearly demonstrating interest, but I was always the first one to turn my eyes away being as shy as I was. It was definitely a heavy-duty crush, something I had never ever felt before. It was exhilarating. I began wishing I would see him each time I left the house. This went on for several weeks before he finally approached me.

At first, I was very afraid to begin a relationship with him since I wondered whether or not he was the more open-minded type who would be accepting of my divorced status and not judging me for it. A divorced woman wasn't someone to bring home to your parents—no matter whether it was her fault or not.

He was very attracted to me, and the feelings in his heart outweighed those thoughts. We started dating and were instantly in a relationship, and before long, we were very much in love.

I had never known the love of a man until then. I felt like life had just begun.

When I told him the details of my divorce, he felt bad and completely understood the circumstances. He also knew that I had no family in New York and quickly took to being it. He was extremely considerate and attentive to my needs, and when I didn't have time to eat—because of work or school—he would bring me meals. He took me on vacations since I had never been anywhere. We were extremely happy together. I lived in complete bliss and felt that all the pain and suffering I had gone through in the past was worth this love. This love made it easy to never look back.

The sun was brighter, the grass seemed greener, the world was beautiful, and I constantly smiled and laughed. Nothing could hurt me, and nothing could make me upset. I was calm, peaceful, and most importantly, I was loved. Even the nightmares I had suffered from for years stopped. Love was incredibly powerful and healing.

It felt like such an unbreakable bond with him. We never argued. One time, when we were on the street in New York City, we stopped to kiss as if no one was in the world except for us. Amid this long kiss, a woman stopped to compliment us. She said that we were such a beautiful couple, and she wished more people would love each other the way that we obviously did. I will never forget that day. It was evident to anyone who was around us. We could just look at each other, and the love would penetrate through us. It was intense.

You know how sometimes couples grow to resemble each other? Well, we already had that. We were also each other's best friend. Anytime we weren't working, we were together. We were inseparable, and we both lost contact with our friends because we were so consumed with each other. It wasn't right, but it's the truth.

It was not just the first time being in love; it was also the first time I ever enjoyed sex. Being loved by this man felt like the most amazing and fulfilling feeling of wholeness. Everything was beautiful. I didn't want anything else but to continue my life this way.

Although I was in complete bliss, I didn't feel any urgency to be married or have children at that time. I didn't even think about it. I was extremely content just being with him.

This love and our union helped me to finally grow into a woman who was very much loved and respected. His love helped me gain confidence in myself, my life, my career, and my future. With love in my life, the world was mine.

However, with our cultural background, nothing was that simple. For almost three years, we had to hide our relationship from everyone. When we wanted to go out, we had to go to places that were farther away, and I would have to duck down in the car until we got out of our neighborhood. He was protecting my reputation. I would have been judged for dating since I was not yet engaged or married to him.

After the third year, without any pressure from me, he decided to tell his relatives about me. Then, like a ton of bricks, my fairy tale started tumbling down. I saw him overcome with sadness and confusion because his relatives told him that he would be ridiculed in the eyes of our culture if he married me since I was considered tainted due to my divorce. Also, the Catholic church wouldn't accept me because of this—and because my father wasn't Catholic.

That damn scarlet letter showed its ugly judgmental face again. I heard screaming in my mind: "There is nothing wrong with me! I don't have leprosy! I was loyal to my culture, and it didn't work out. Must I pay for it for the rest of my life!?"

I felt that he shouldn't have told me what they said to him and handled it like a man by defending us and defending me.

Their ignorance and judgments against me did upset me, but they would never break the bond I had with him. Their shallow opinions should never sway his devotion to me. They had never met me or even considered how happy we were together. It was always about what people would say or think.

Who the hell were these people to judge me by my misfortunes and not value my integrity as a woman? I was furious and insulted. I had been through enough. I deserved this love!

The most outrageous part was that I realized they weren't as much of the problem as he was. For the next few weeks, he was visibly distraught about their opinions. I felt like their opinions actually began to outweigh the value of our union. I was in utter shock to learn that he was one of them. He actually cared about the opinions of others, which meant he shared the same mentality: a lot of mouth and no balls!

Cultural codes outweighed love for him. It made him seem less masculine and more emotionally driven; it was a direct insult to his manhood. For me, his reaction was a direct insult.

I was beside myself. I didn't know this side of him. I was devastated, upset, and uncertain about his courage as a man. He knew me better than anyone. *How could their opinions matter more than our love?* If I loved someone and the whole world was opposed to him, I would never leave him. I saw him in a whole new light. He lacked the courage to go up against our opposition and fight for us. I also realized that this would be the beginning of more family influences spilling into and wreaking havoc on our personal lives since those judgmental relatives would be a part of our lives.

This experience made me see what he was really made of. He was not a strong man, and he was easily manipulated. The fact that he allowed their opinions to make him doubt whether he could be with me demonstrated a weakness about him that was a huge turnoff. I wanted to share my life with a man and not a coward who would leave me if persuaded to. So, I took every ounce of courage in me and decided to lead with my mind and break up with him.

One evening, he stayed in his car for the entire night in front of my apartment because coming in was no longer an option. Other times, I would find flowers and gifts at my door when I came home. It was all pointless and hurt me more. He was showing me love in the weakest ways. Fight for your woman with actions—not gifts!

He said, "You could live 150 years, and no one will ever love you more than I do."

I thought, *Wow! To feel that way about a woman and* still *have no balls to fight for her just confirms what a coward he is.* I was done.

I was devastated for a very long time after the breakup. We were still very much in love and never imagined being with someone else. I cried nonstop for months, obsessively listening to Toni Braxton's "Another Sad Love Song."

It was my first heartbreak; I never knew that kind of pain before. I felt like I had been dropped from the top of a building, survived with broken bones throughout my body, and given no painkillers. *That* is how much it hurt to go through. I remember describing the pain with these exact words: "It would have hurt less if he died. At least I would have known that his death was why we couldn't be together—not because he allowed our relationship to die because he was a coward." The breakup was worse than mourning his death.

Several painful months later, he contacted me. He was completely miserable without me, and he realized that he was wrong. He wanted us to reunite and be married, but it was too late. At that point, I resented him so much for the immense pain he had put me through that I could not accept that it took him so long to realize my worth. I didn't think I would be able to respect him again. The damage was done. I had to move on. It was incredibly difficult but necessary.

A year or so later, he married a girl who his family had selected for him. A few days before his wedding, we spoke on the phone, both of us crying, and he told me that he would be wishing that she was me standing next to him on their wedding day. That statement meant that cultural code had won over his manhood. He would live his life as a prisoner—without true love—for the sake of cultural views and beliefs. Been there, done that. At that point, he made it easier for me to move on. I had no regrets about my decision.

In conclusion, I would rather have loved than not, and even after such heartache, the two years and nine months in that relationship were the happiest I have ever been in my life.

That breakup definitely caused some deep emotional damage that I still carry in some way today. It was such a heavy blow to my self-worth. I did not deserve to have that love taken away from me because of my tainted reputation in my community. I felt constantly punished in my life.

The Scorpio

To my surprise, I learned you *can* fall in love again. It happened less than a year later, but this time, it was with the complete opposite of the previous one. Our relationship was like a movie where a good girl and a bad boy fall in love. Inevitable disaster?

I was an independent young lady, but I was still naive about the world. With natural brown hair that flowed down to my waist, minimal makeup, nicely tanned, slim, and tall (five foot eight), I was probably sexy in a nerdy way. I had just finished college and started on my career path. I was determined, self-sufficient, and self-respecting. I was a girl whose past could not be seen through the way I carried myself. My focus was only on moving forward.

He was soft-spoken, and mysterious. He had dark blond hair, blue eyes, and an intense gaze. He was much, much wiser to the world than I was. He was a bad boy whose presence alone shot electric bolts through my body every time I saw him. I thought he was the most beautiful man I had ever seen—he was often told that he resembled James Dean—but that was not what took me over. Even before speaking to him, I felt a deep connection with him. I felt like his heart had words only for me. I needed to find out why.

He had a quiet, private demeanor, and he seemed to possess so much depth. I was very much attracted to the deeper, quiet part of him, which I believed not many people could see. To me, he was transparent. I felt like he carried a lot of pain inside and only suffered in private, keeping everyone at a distance to keep them from seeing his pain or causing more. I was very much like him in that way. It was like we were the same kind of person. I wanted to share our secret worlds together.

I was extremely attracted to him on many levels. I was too young and lovestruck to care about his reputation or how he made his money. Normally, that alone would have me running the other way, but I just couldn't. I wanted nothing more than to be his. He was my kryptonite.

He was also of the same nationality. We were both rebels in our culture. We were both divorced. We were both judged. He used to work several hours a week, but after the divorce and an infant child, he decided to find quicker ways to make money.

At first, I thought he would never be interested in me. I was a nerd, and he was the neighborhood bad boy who a lot of girls had a crush on. To my surprise, he quietly approached me one day with that all-so-famous line: "Do I know you from somewhere?" He was so intrigued that he insisted we hang out right away. I was with a friend, and so was he. Completely out of my character, I agreed. We all went to a diner, and later that evening, he came back to pick us up and take us to a popular nightclub in New York City. He was known by many people there, and as soon as we got to the door, they let us in—without waiting in line. We sat in the VIP section. I hadn't been to clubs much and did not even know how to dress. I was clearly underdressed. My innocence was screaming at him, but I think he was intrigued by it.

He spoke in my ear nonstop the entire night because the music was so loud. I couldn't even hear most of his conversation, but I loved feeling his breath on my neck. When we left, his friend told me that he had never seen him speak that much to anyone. He was a quiet, almost secretive type, but we had an instant magnetic attraction and an intense chemistry.

I fell hard and fast. There was no running from that type of connection. It drew me in like a magnet. I was under his spell for years. I was convinced that he was the man I was born for. I loved him dangerously. He presented a challenge and a risk, and although I wasn't a risk-taker, nothing stopped me.

He didn't care about my divorce or cultural codes. The third time he took me out, we returned late—and he slept over for the first time. I don't know what he expected, but I offered him the bed as I slept on the sofa. I think he was completely dumbfounded by this and realized he was dealing with an entirely different type of woman than he was used to. I was strictly a relationship type of girl. After that, he seemed to move forward cautiously with baby steps. We still saw each other, but we didn't kiss or become intimate for several months. To be precise, we met in July, and we finally became an item on New Year's Day.

Due to his lifestyle and always being away doing "things" to make a living, I only saw him a few times a year. He knew that he completely owned me and that I would wait forever for him. As the years went by, I became restless, but he assured me by saying, "Give me some more time to set things straight in my life. Don't worry. You will get tired of seeing me every day." Those words softened me and gave me incredible patience to continue to wait.

He was struggling to try to change his life and start a new one with me. Since I had no greater desire than to be his, I was willing to move anywhere just to be with him. I patiently waited another year, and then another, finally turning into seven.

For almost a decade, my eyes saw nothing but him. I had no peripheral vision. I went through those years with very little recollection of anything except work and the few times we were together. I was in a daze for years—just working and waiting—and I didn't even think of the possibility of being with anyone else or giving another man a chance to breathe my way. Even when he wasn't next to me, I was completely consumed by him. I heard rumors in the neighborhood that he was with other women, but I could not leave him. I called it quits with him several times because I felt like a damn fool, waiting for him while he was saving me for marriage, yet was out enjoying whatever else he could in the meantime. But I was in too deep. I had no desire for any other man on the planet. I had lost myself.

The ending to this already tragic love story? He had been going back and forth to Europe for several months at a time to rebuild his parent's home. During this time, he called me often. He was making a lot of changes to his life, and he was trying to prepare for our life together. He was finally ready to settle down, and I was beyond thrilled. However, instead, I got some very disturbing news. A friend of mine heard that a woman we knew of was going around telling people she was pregnant with his child. Apparently, it happened several months before he left for Europe. I could not breathe, and my whole body started to tremble. I immediately called him in Europe to confirm it. He said that he received the same news, he admitted his affair with her, and he told me that she assured him before he left that she had gotten an abortion, but she lied to try to trap him. I knew of his affair with her for some time. He told me that she was obsessed with him, but it was over. I knew she would use the baby to manipulate him and cause a lot of trouble in his life. She was the opposite of me on every level: low morals, big mouth, troublemaker, drama. I knew that I wanted nothing to do with him if he shared a child with her.

I devoted the best years of my youth to this man, and within a minute, my hopes and dreams were crushed. I told him that I could not be a part of it anymore. Out of character, feeling desperate and hopeless, his masculine wall came down. He quickly replied, "Please don't leave me now."

However, I finally did. It was the straw that broke the camel's back, but more importantly, I was also almost a decade older. I was much wiser and less dreamy.

I finally accepted that he never deserved the level of my devotion and loyalty, but my love—or addiction—for him didn't die so easily.

I had to cut all ties to this self-destructive relationship. I moved to a whole new town, a new borough, where I knew no one, just to avoid seeing him. I desperately needed to gain the ability to open my eyes beyond him, see the world that I had blinded myself to, and try to live past the lost years.

I had focused all my energy on my career and quickly climbed the ladder and excelled.

A couple of years later, his fate was even more interesting. He had been convicted of breaking the law and was deported back to Europe where he was born. *What kind of life would I have had if I had stayed with him? Thank you, God, for protecting me. If only I loved God as much as I loved him, I would have not suffered so.*

Looking back years later, through age and wisdom, I cannot see one single thing about him that was worth waiting and sacrificing myself for. Where was my self-worth? I completely used my heart instead of my head. I had lost the best years of my twenties and early thirties waiting for Mr. Wrong.

Ignorant? Young and stupid? Blinded by love? Whatever you want to call it, it was what it was: a lesson in life and a lesson in love.

That was my second devastating heartbreak. I couldn't imagine ever living through another one or falling in love again.

In hindsight, I know that I should never think too much or give myself that intensely to anyone. I had become a prisoner to myself and my happiness because I felt incomplete without him. I felt like I couldn't enjoy my life unless he was a part of it, yet he offered me nothing. I was so incredibly stupid.

All that time spent thinking and waiting for him was time wasted. In this case, it was years where my only focus was him—hours of the day, sleepless nights, weeks of yearning, months of loneliness—only to find out later that I was a damn fool.

Was it love or lust—and how can we know the difference when they feel the same?

I summed up this whole relationship with one question: Is love enough? And the answer is no.

The Aries

I met him a year or so after the passing of my brother. I was still not myself. I was grieving, vulnerable, lonely, weak, lost, and heartbroken.

He was strong, confident, hardworking, and handsome, but I interpreted his desire to control every aspect of my life as him wanting to take care of me. He literally wouldn't even let me pay for my own gas. At first, I believed it was culturally based to not to let a woman pay for anything, and a large part of it may have been, but with him, it was also control.

Every moment I wasn't working, he spent with me. I thought it was because he was in love with me, and some of it may have been that, but I later realized he was purposely alienating me from my friends.

My best friend warned me that his behavior was worrisome, but I felt the need for him at that time in my life. He was always there for me. I felt safe and protected, but I was never able to love him. He wasn't gentle at all. He was kind of like a caveman in many aspects. When we were walking in the street, instead of holding my hand, he would sometimes hold on to my arm! Who does that? I would always remove it and give him a puzzled look like, "WTF are you doing?" It was clearly a control thing to hold onto me like I was his possession.

In time, it became apparent that his need for control was extreme, and I began to worry.

One afternoon, about a year into this relationship, a friend called me to invite me to sing at an annual ethnic concert. I had loved singing and performing since I was a child, and I accepted the invitation.

Consumed with excitement, after I hung up, I started telling him about it while we were crossing the street. Suddenly, completely unexpectedly, he delivered a burning slap right across my face in the middle of the road, leaving me in utter shock.

I was numb, not to mention completely humiliated in front of all the people stopped at the red light on both sides of the road who witnessed it. Instantly, slow-motioned flashbacks flooded my head as my mind pulled me to that once-familiar feeling of physical abuse from my marriage. *Dear Lord,* I thought. *Am I back in this type of relationship again?*

Apparently, he was extremely old-fashioned and strict with cultural beliefs and believed a woman's job was to be a wife and mother and *not* a performer. He saw it as disgraceful that I would be excited about such a thing. Early in our relationship, he pretended not to be old-fashioned. He knew that I was very open-minded and modern. He clearly took off his mask and proved the opposite.

Instantly, I told him that this relationship was over, that he was sick in his head, and that I would never tolerate physical abuse again in my life!

As if he could force me to be with him, he told me that it wasn't a choice I could make. He said that he wouldn't let me break up with him. He said I was lucky that he had accepted me since I was already divorced, had boyfriends, was a bit older than him, and no one else from our culture would want me. *The scarlet letter resurfaces,* I thought. He said if I behaved properly, then he would never need to hit me. *What a barbarian!*

He consumed every part of my life, which made it nearly impossible to get away from him. I finally saw his true colors and the sick monster that he really was. I feared being with him, but I especially feared attempting to escape. He clearly saw that I had no feelings for him at all, but he purchased tickets for us to take a vacation in hopes of reviving me. I was afraid of what he would do to me if I refused to go. You may not be able to understand this, but trust me, I knew I had to obey until I devised a safe way to terminate this union. I knew I couldn't fight aggression with aggression.

While on vacation, I was looking to purchase a bikini. While I was in the dressing room, he told me to steal it—but I refused. After I paid for it, we left the store and began walking toward the parking lot. Once again, completely unexpectedly, he hit me across the face for not obeying him.

I immediately started running into the street without looking and almost got hit by a speeding car that came within inches of my body. God saved me! When I got to the other side, I fell to the ground and caught my breath. I couldn't believe I had almost died while trying to run away from this man. When I looked back in his direction, I knew I was his prisoner. I couldn't leave. I feared him more than the police. He was relentless and very strong, and he controlled my every move. I knew I had to plan an escape because I knew that he would never let me leave.

It was an especially difficult few years since I was grieving the loss of my brother and had found myself in another abusive relationship. I lived in fear and was very sad and anxious.

I devised an escape plan. I found a basement apartment in a different borough and literally started moving my belongings by car at night while he worked. I took several trips to my undisclosed location and later had my friends move the rest of my furniture. I finally escaped, but I lived in constant fear of what he would do if he found me.

Unsurprisingly, he stalked me and showed up at the hospital where I worked. I had to take alternate ways home every day, constantly checking rearview mirrors, making certain he wasn't following me, and hoping he wouldn't find out where I now lived.

Being stalked was a sickening feeling, and it went on for several months. I always felt uneasy. I even slept in fear. No one could help me. I knew he didn't fear the police, and they wouldn't help.

He called me nonstop. I wouldn't answer, but then he started calling me constantly and disrupting me at work. Luckily, I was the supervisor and controlled the calls. I didn't want my workers to see that my personal life was a mess; therefore, I spoke to him, but I insisted that I would never get back together with him. He pleaded and promised that he would "let" me have my friends back and that he would change and spoke of marriage.

Oh, how the tables have turned! Recall that he previously said that "I was lucky" because no one would want me because of my past, and now he was begging to be with me? *Who's the unwanted bitch now?*

I kept denying his request with a 1,000,000 percent conviction. He was relentless, insisted he had changed, and begged me to meet up with him to talk. Finally, I agreed to meet with him in hopes that I can convince him in person that I wanted nothing to do with him. I hoped he would finally leave me alone.

We sat in the car when we met that night. For at least an hour, he was extremely persistent and wouldn't take no for an answer. I was exhausted, so, thinking that it would help, I decided to lie to him and tell him that I had met someone else and that we should both just move on. Instead, he punched me in my jaw! I saw stars. It hurt like hell. I thought he broke it. I couldn't close it or speak for what felt like several minutes. I just kept moaning in pain, tears streaming down my face, as I sat there feeling hopeless. I thought, *Why do I have so much bad luck in my life?* When I thought about my family being so far away and what they would think if they saw me in this pitiful condition, I cried even harder.

By some miracle, after this incident, he left me alone. I was finally free. Sometime after he went to Europe and got arranged to someone—happy for me, sad for her.

This relationship and the past up to that point left me feeling lost and bruised. All I wanted was a loving life partner, but I kept ending up in bad relationships. I was so tired of everything I had endured up to that point. I needed to re-center myself, figure things out, and learn to be happy again. So, after that relationship, I remained single for several years. I focused on myself personally, professionally, and artistically.

I spent more time with friends, took vacations, and recharged my soul. In time, I became healthy and happy again. I told myself it never happened, and I moved on. It was the same mechanism I had used for my arranged marriage. Pretending it never happened and keep moving always worked for me.

I also started gravitating toward singing and songwriting.

The Gemini

I was heaven, and he was hell. We were the angel and the devil. At first, we were just friends. I met him at a club. He was charming and simple, but I remembered seeing a coldness when I looked into his eyes. It was almost like his soul was empty. His easygoing nature made transitioning from friendship to being in a relationship happen effortlessly. I felt no pressure or control from him at all. He gave me space and freedom since he was also free-spirited. We both had no relatives in New York. He was also divorced and of the same background, but he held no cultural beliefs at all. He was even more open-minded than I was.

I let him move in with me temporarily because he told me that his lease was up soon. He said he was looking for another place. Yeah, right. I was so naïve. However, I did say, "It's only temporary."

The first couple of months were very easy and lighthearted. He was kind and gentle. He made me laugh, helped around the apartment, and cooked meals for us. I felt like he was my buddy more than anything else. He was not the romantic type at all. I wasn't in love with him, and I didn't feel any passion with him—since kissing him was like kissing a doorknob—but I was content. He was what I thought I needed at the time. Simple.

Long story short, things started to change quickly—or unveil—and his dark side began surfacing. Within a few months, he started to go missing for several days at a time. I honestly thought he was having an affair until he finally confessed that his affair was cocaine. I grew up sheltered and was not exposed to drugs or anyone with an addiction. I didn't know how to handle it.

When he went missing, he wouldn't answer my calls for days. I couldn't sleep. I stayed in bed all night, crying my eyes out and wondering why he was torturing me. I felt abandoned and unloved again. I went to work unfocused, exhausted, and sad every day.

I spent several hours a week alone on a church bench, crying hysterically, seeking God, and begging for His help.

I did a significant amount of emotional writing during this relationship. It was my only outlet since I was too embarrassed to tell anyone how I was being treated, or I should say, how I *allowed* myself to be treated. I thought he would be different than the others; instead, I found myself in another bad relationship.

With his lifestyle came the need to constantly lie to cover up. Since I have zero tolerance for dishonesty or secrets in any relationship, his lies literally tortured me. When he was out on his binges and doing God knows what else, he was unreachable. His cell phone was turned off for days at a time. When he returned home, he always had the same story. He swore that he wasn't having an affair and that he was just hanging out with his friends.

I kept pleading to him and asking, "Why are you putting me through this?"

Although he saw that his actions were torturing me, he continued to do it several times a month. I literally had a calendar of how many days he did not come home, marked with an X. They were up to fourteen a month. I couldn't understand what he was doing. I was good to him. I didn't deserve such suffering.

I loathe injustice as much as dishonesty and feeling used or abused. I was mentally beaten and tested to the point of raw anger. I became so verbally abusive to him when he *did* come home that I recall him saying to me that my words could kill a horse. I felt such deep, undeserving pain that I wanted to inflict it back, tenfold. He never verbally or physically abused me, but his behavior was emotionally abusive.

Since I couldn't handle another failed relationship, I did everything to salvage it. However, it became clear that I needed to give up since there was absolutely nothing to salvage there. He was the complete opposite of who I was. He was an ugly person with no remorse for his actions or how he treated people. That coldness that I saw in his eyes the first time we met was very clear now. He was a pathological liar. He had no compassion, he was ruthless, and he lived only for his own gain.

Being with him was destroying my mental status. I knew I would just continue to bury myself in a ditch if I stayed. Living with his compulsive lies and torment created trust issues I had to work on for years. From him, I learned how not to be so damn honest all the time—not everyone deserves it.

After almost two years, I got his belongings together and threw his ass out! It was the very first time I saw him cry or show any emotions, but I did not become sympathetic. To me, he was a crocodile. He had to live with his demons elsewhere. He tortured me to the maximum. I needed his extreme toxicity out of my life.

I've come to learn that he was a con artist of sorts and owed large sums of money to several people. Apparently, I was the last person to know who he really was. I really disliked that part of my trusting and naïve nature. It made me an easy target for evil people. I was his perfect prey.

Luckily, I was never in love with him. It was the feeling of failure that took me down. It hurt differently—not less, just different.

The tolls of the past weighed me down greatly, and I eventually fell into depression. It was a dark place I hadn't known before. I couldn't climb out of it as easily as I had been able to in the past. It was a deeper level of sadness than I had known; my soul was crying. I mourned my own ignorance and mistakes. I spent up to ten hours a week in a chapel, connecting with God and praying for guidance and clarity.

I found a small, simple-to-read prayer book, *My Daily Bread*, which became my first course in learning about religion and God's Word. The words brought peace to me and an understanding of the way we are expected to live while on the earth. I read it often to cope with my pain. It was the true first chapter of my own spiritual education and growth. It was comforting and warmly welcomed.

Queen of a Broken Heart

Sincerity has been my enemy.
Honesty has brought me pain.
As many times as my heart has bled,
that many times I have tried again,
not giving up on love,
or the belief that it does exist.

Take away all that I have and all that I own,
just give me inner peace and love.
Without it, we are nothing but empty souls.
Nothing else can be a substitute,
for it is real while everything else is not.

The Taurus

I finally found him—or did I? Just thinking about it exhausts me.

I felt a deep, intense emotional connection, mutual love, and respect with a very Americanized man. He was from the same culture, but he was living a modern lifestyle, which was exactly the way I wanted to live.

He was handsome, clean-cut, hardworking, honest, and very romantic. He played and coached little league soccer during his free time. One day, he invited me to come with him. On the way to the field, he played a song for me that he said reminded him of me. As I listened, I felt like I was floating. It was about a girl with heartbreak and pain, and the guy was singing to her about how he wanted to be the one to heal her. I wish I remember who sang it.

We fell in love fast and hard. We were extremely compatible. We hardly ever slept because we would stay up for hours talking. We completely lost track of time. It wasn't even a sexual relationship. I believed that he was my forever man. I was convinced that all the previous bad relationships had led me to him.

Every single aspect of us was perfect and too good to be true. My mind started doubting this perfection because I was so used to failure. *Is this for real—or are we both living our hopes and creating these feelings?* I prayed desperately: "Dear God, please keep us together and always happy. I am so afraid. If you are planning to take him away from me, take him from me now because I won't want to live without him if this continues the way it has."

Several weeks later, he mentioned to me that his parents might have something negative to say if they knew he was dating a divorced woman who was a bit older than he was. There it was again; the scarlet letter was back to haunt me several years later. *Am I dealing with another man who will be persuaded by it?* I was upset, hurt, and insulted, but I held it inside and remained silent. I felt scared and unstable. I had already lost a man I was in love with to it (The Libra), and I knew I could not handle another such heartbreak.

We had an extraordinary relationship with mutual love and understanding that is rare to find. I thought, *If we lose each other, we definitely won't find a bond like this again.* I was certain of it. I prayed that he would be a stronger man and not let ignorance influence our bond. Although we didn't speak of it again, it remained in the back of my mind. I was afraid of losing him to it.

To my utter surprise, as time went on, a much larger problem surfaced. Apparently, we had a bigger enemy to worry about. He had a ghost in his closet. It was alcohol, but I was too lovestruck or oblivious to realize it at first.

We were together for only a couple of months, but every time we went out, he would take me to several bars. I was not a bar type of girl. I didn't care to drink, but since I loved him, I never complained or thought it was an issue. I was just happy to be together. I just thought he liked bars, but this pattern of barhopping defined him.

He became belligerent when he drank, which was the complete opposite of who he was when he was sober. I had never had any experience with alcoholism before, but he proved that he loved his liquor more than he loved me.

He proved this on our last night together. We went out to dinner, and he consumed way too much, got very drunk, and became angry. I refused to let him drive and insisted on driving home, but he refused to give me the keys. This turned into our first argument. Knowing how much he loved me, I told him that if he got into the car to drive, our relationship would be over. I never thought for a second that he would. Without hesitation, the stubborn mule got up, left me at the restaurant, got in his car, and drove off!

I was pissed! I was also afraid that he would hurt or kill someone while he was driving drunk. A flood of emotions and thoughts instantly overwhelmed me. *Would this would be our life together?* Then I remembered that love isn't enough (the Scorpio lesson).

A few minutes later, on my cab ride home, he started calling my cell phone nonstop. Also stubborn and now fuming, I refused to answer. He had a chance to do the right thing and show his devotion to me, but he didn't. Instead, he abandoned me and made me feel worthless. I was so upset that I did not want to hear whatever he had to say.

His drinking problem and the conversation about the opinions of his relatives started to play back in my mind. A negative thought pattern followed. I was flooded with memories of past failed relationships. I thought, *Should I again attempt to stay in a relationship that I may eventually lose to destructive addiction, cultural beliefs, or both? If I believe it is going to end eventually, it should end now.* My heart was already in deep, but I couldn't handle it being any more broken.

When I got home, he was waiting for me outside of my place. I was very afraid because of the look of rage in his eyes. I thought he would hit me. I cautiously passed him by, went into my apartment, locked the door, and never called him again.

Truth be told, I never wanted to end our relationship. I was hoping he would seek some sort of help and return to me. I didn't want him to be an alcoholic. He was so nasty and mean when he drank. I needed to know that I was safe and secure, and I wanted him to assure me of our future together, but he never did. It was truly over. Looks like alcohol was his true love.

When this short-lived love story ended, I went back to the chapel I frequented during my most difficult times. For years, I had sat in one of the front benches, but this time, I sat all the way in the back. I fell to my knees and wept my heart out, feeling like I had just lost the last chance for true love and any hope for happiness.

It was a different kind of crying than my first heartbreak. It was followed by moans that came from deep within—a sum of all the pain and hardship in my life. I couldn't take any more. I was raw inside. My heart had been broken before, but this time, after many disappointments and feelings of hopelessness, I felt shattered. It felt like the pain of a hundred cuts at once.

I've sometimes wondered if I made a mistake in that relationship. Should I have stayed and worked out his drinking issues? Did I use it as an excuse to escape another possible failure? Had I become self-destructive? Was I now petrified of love? Was it the right thing to do? I didn't know anymore.

The opposite of love is fear. I had become afraid of the element that I needed the most: love. Was I at a point where I quit too easily because of the fear of failure? Was I so used to it that I subconsciously expected it? Did I use the law of attraction to create it? Or was I just overthinking things?

I remained single for a couple of years after that. My heart was cold. Love was no longer real. Hope was dying.

The Wall

The wall is up; you cannot hurt me now.
You cannot see or touch my scars.
I remain closed and refuse to let you in.
I pretend to be distant and cold.
In reality, I am afraid to bleed again.

So many heartaches and disappointments,
So many scars of the past,
So many bruises not yet healed,
Left without trust or even hope,
Left feeling empty, frightened, and alone.

Break it down, take it down, feel the warmth.
Take it down, let it crumble, set my soul free.
Let me live in your heart where I can breathe.
Set me free, let me fly, knowing that you love me.

The wall of protection that we build around us.
If we don't let anyone in our hearts, how can they love us?
What must it take for us to feel safe again?

The element we need the most is sometimes
that which we fear the most.
Afraid to love but wanting and needing it more than anything else.

I Will Love Again

As time passes and life goes on,
I sit and think, Where did I go wrong?
You were the one who filled my heart.
How will I go on now that we are apart?

I felt like a child, so happy and free.
With you by my side, nothing could hurt me.
Now my soul yearns for your gentle touch—
If only you could have loved me this much.

My eyes are open, but I cannot see.
My heart is beating, but I have died.
I believed in love, but it has killed me.

I am told a person can love again.
I have tried and found I only pretend.
None of them compared to you.
My love for them was never true.

Eyes opened or closed, you are all that I see.
You were the one who completed me.
I will accept and heal and move on.
I will love again—even though you're gone.

The Sagittarius

I was seeking stability in the unstable. I met him at a wedding when we were just teenagers. We knew a lot of the same people, and I had seen him around through the years. He was Americanized and not culturally driven at all. He was very good-looking, in great shape, and always seemed very polite. Women were gaga over him, but he was not my type at all. He was obnoxious and laughed ten times louder than the average person. I felt like he was lacking some sort of attention.

Truth be told, I never liked him in a romantic way. He was just a friend, and I didn't feel capable of true love again after my past ordeals. However, my girlfriends told me I would "learn" to love him, and they strongly suggested being with a man who loved me more than I loved him. After what I'd been through, I thought it might be a wise choice, and I allowed myself to be in a relationship with him when he continuously pursued me. After a few months, I realized I was in another type of hell.

This story should be a movie and is worth sharing.

A mutual friend was terminally ill, and I would visit him every day after work at the hospital. He and his wife were close friends of mine, and I would go stay with him after work so that she could get some sleep. The Sagittarius, who I hadn't seen in almost a decade, would also often visit him, and we chatted during his visits, but I thought nothing of it. After a few weeks, he told me that he was falling in love with me after seeing how I cared for our dying friend. Later, he confessed that most of his visits were really to see me. I didn't see that as a compliment at all since our mutual friend needed the attention—not me.

For weeks, he pursued me in a romantic manner. He sent me flowers, showed up at my job with lunch, and bought the whole staff coffee and donuts. He made friends with my friends and coworkers, and they said I was crazy not to give him a chance. Although I found it overwhelming at the time, I thought he *would* always take care of me. I also believed I would never fall in love again so this would probably be a wise choice. I went against my heart—since it was broken and betrayed—and I chose logic instead.

He would often buy me expensive gifts for no reason, but I did not like it because it made me feel like he was trying to buy my love. It made me very uncomfortable. I asked him to please stop, but he continued to do so. I started to wonder how he really earned his money. He often pretended to be more than who he was to people.

I even overheard him lying to a friend of mine that he owned a popular club in the neighborhood, but I personally knew the real owner. That was a big turnoff, and I called him out on it.

He lacked a lot of qualities that I wanted from a man. He became less and less desirable to me. I felt no love or respect for him, and it was pointless. Finally, I told him that we could remain friends, but I couldn't be in a relationship with him.

Instead, the gifts got more expensive. I was completely insulted, and he could never understand why. I did not want his gifts, and I did not want him. I was not for sale! He was an insult to the woman I was.

I was contemplating an easy way to get out of this so-called relationship when he reminded me that Valentine's Day was coming soon—and I should be ready for a proposal. I felt my insides turn and instantly responded, "Don't even think about it!" I had already made it clear that I wanted out. *Why the hell would I marry him?* He looked at me in shock and reminded me that most girls would love to be in my position, and culturally—since I was over thirty, divorced, and expected to be married already—I should be lucky to be proposed to by a younger man who had never been married.

I had never been desperate enough to marry for status. Thank God!

Enough was enough. I attempted to break up with him civilly, but he got very angry and turned into something like the Incredible Hulk character. The scary transition took place in seconds. It was like he was schizophrenic. I was frightened and slowly tried to leave his apartment. He grabbed me, dragged me away from the door, threw me on the floor, and took my purse, car keys, and phone. He locked me inside his apartment and left me there for hours. His apartment door could only be opened with a key from either side. It was located on the second floor, and there was no fire escape. Since it was too high to jump out of the window, I sat and waited as his captive—not knowing what he was going to do next. It was unbelievable.

When he finally came back several hours later, I was furious. I told him that he couldn't force me to stay with him and to let me go. He would not let me leave, and he was too strong to fight.

After hours of pleading, exhausted, I passed out and fell asleep.

In the middle of the night, I opened my eyes and saw him about a foot away from my face, staring at me in the dark. I was frightened out of my skin. He looked like a crazy person, and I had no idea how long he had been staring at me. Somehow, I played it cool and said, "Go to sleep. We had a rough day." I turned away from him and pretended to go back to sleep. Instead I started to plan how I could get away from him.

In the morning, I decided to play polite and abide by his rules, and pretended to agree that we should continue to be in a relationship, and it worked. I relaxed him enough to let me go home. A few minutes later, as I was driving on the highway, his car approached mine. I immediately accelerated and tried to lose him. He got violent and aggressively tried to run me off the road. I was shaking like a leaf. Finally, I saw a police car getting off an exit, and I started beeping my horn frantically to stop them for help. When he saw this, he sped away. I got off the exit where the police car went, but I couldn't find it.

I drove home but didn't feel safe, and I couldn't sleep at a friend's place because I didn't want to give anyone problems. I double-checked all the windows and the door. I felt very frightened and alone.

In the middle of the night, I was awakened to the sound of banging and ripping on my bedroom window. I jumped out of bed and looked outside, and he was standing there with the look of the devil and white spit/foam at the corners of his mouth. He had a long wooden object in his hand that he had used to rip through my screen window. Thankfully it was too high to climb without a ladder.

I anxiously called security and begged them to come quickly. In my mind, I didn't think anyone could stop him. He was crazy. Security came quickly, but there was no sign of him. I didn't believe he was gone and did not sleep at all the rest of the night—or for days to follow. My eyes grew dark and heavy. I was functioning like a zombie. I felt like I had no one who could help me. I was just hoping he would give up and move on.

How the hell do I attract these types of men?

After a few days, he started to call me, but at first, I would not answer. Since I didn't want to continue to live in fear, I eventually answered to see where his mind was and to try to reason with him. Reasoning with a crazy man is crazy, but I was desperate.

He insisted that he wanted the mattress back. A few weeks before, I had nonchalantly mentioned in a conversation that I was going to buy a new mattress. Out of the blue, the following day, he showed up with a truck in front of my apartment and delivered a mattress to my home. I wasn't happy about his outrageous antics of trying to buy love, but it was easier to accept it then to anger him.

On the phone, he told me that he had several thousands of dollars in money and jewelry secretly sown into the mattress and needed to come to pick it up as soon as possible.

I thought, *Are they stolen goods!? Does having them in my home make me an accomplice!?* I did not want him in my apartment or anywhere near me, and I did not want anything that belonged to him.

Sleep-deprived and scared shitless, I took a knife and cut the queen-sized mattress to shreds until there were no spaces left uncut. All that was left was wood and springs; ripped cloths and sponges were all over my bedroom floor. Picture what it was like sneaking out that shredded queen-sized mattress out to the dumpster during the night so no one could see me.

I was satisfied to find that there was nothing hidden in that mattress! *He lied to try to get into my apartment? Very scary and manipulative.* I felt relieved that I wasn't tied to him in any way. I let him know what I did and called his bluff.

I couldn't help but wonder what he would have done to me if I had let him in.

He was quiet for a few days, but I didn't believe it was over. I was afraid of being alone in my apartment. Out of desperation, I finally told one of my best friends everything in case something did happen to me.

There was still to be no peace. For the next few weeks, he strangely appeared at every single place I went. He did not make a public scene. He just showed his face and then left before I did. I felt like I was losing my mind. I couldn't understand the coincidence of his presence everywhere I went. I felt on edge and was afraid that he would hurt me.

The feeling of being stalked can make you lose your mind. You anxiously and constantly look behind your back with every turn you make. I had been stalked in a previous relationship, and it was just as disturbing (The Aries). My heart was racing out of my chest.

At work, I started obsessing over these occurrences—and a thought came to my mind. I immediately ran to the parking lot where my car was parked, climbed under my car and saw a magnetic box attached to the bottom of my car. It apparently was a tracking device!

I was sickened and thought about attaching it to a taxi cab and letting him go crazy following that for a while.

Later that evening, I decided I was going to take it to the police station. I couldn't live in fear anymore.

In a last-moment decision, from in front of the station, I called him and told him that I was going to report him and give the tracking device to the cops.

He panicked and shouted "No! You can't do that! A lot of my friends used it before, and there is a lot of information on it that can have them go to jail for years!"

I immediately responded, "You should've thought about that before you decided to stalk me!" I hung up, and a flood of questions filled my head: *Is my life in danger? Is he a part of the Mafia? Would I be killed if they knew I had this in my possession? What should I do? God help me now.*

He must've immediately called one of these friends because shortly after, I received a threatening call from a very angry man who told me I would be a dead person if I went into the police station.

That was not the first time my life had been threatened. Remember, I had been held at gunpoint by my ex-husband. Those thoughts and my current situation made me feel very angry. I was tired of being a victim to bad people. I was driven to the edge and immediately yelled, "Fuck you! Come kill me! You tough guys lent it to him to stalk a woman like little bitches!" I hung up on him. I didn't know where that courage—or insanity—came from, but I was just fucking tired of my unfair life.

They both kept calling nonstop, but I just kept ignoring their calls and sat anxiously in my car, not knowing what to do next.

I had been through so much in my life that I was too numb to be afraid. A part of me felt like I was in charge now. I thought, *Let them panic for a while for torturing me for the past several weeks.*

I fell into a trance. I felt like I was in a Mafia movie where someone had to die at the end. I thought of my family, and tears started streaming down my face. I felt a heavy pain in my chest. It had been extremely hard to raise myself on the streets of New York City without my family.

Moments later, I made a decision. I answered his friend's call and made a bargain with him. I told him that if I returned the device, he would have to promise to keep my ex away from me. He accepted, but I would have to return it immediately. I didn't trust him and feared my life, but I had no choice.

I drove over to my ex's apartment, and he was waiting outside for me. I put the device in a black plastic bag and drove slowly down his dark street, fearing that it was a trap. I stopped the car several feet before where he stood and slowly started walking toward him, making sure not to get too close. He seemed just as anxious as I did, which made me believe that his life was threatened also. I yelled out to him, before handing it over, that he was to promise me that he would leave me alone from that moment on. When he agreed, I threw the device at him, ran back to my car as quickly as I could, and drove away in reverse.

For days, I lived in emotional unrest. I still felt like my life was in danger, and I finally went to see a detective I knew. My family needed to know the truth in case something happened to me.

When the detective ran a report on my ex's name, he said that he thought the printer was malfunctioning when it printed out several pages of charges. He said, "What is a girl like you doing with someone like him?"

I felt embarrassed and ashamed. I had a good reputation in my community and always had a strong, commendable professional life, but my personal life was the complete opposite. I was embarrassed about having any association with such a man and being in that predicament, which was why I avoided going to see this detective in the first place.

It turned out that the detective knew of a "close friend" of my ex's and asked him to come down to the station to talk. The detective informed him that he was aware of what transpired and explained that I was not to be harmed. They came to an agreement, and I finally felt safe enough to go on with my life.

After a while, I was comforted in hearing that he was in a new relationship and that his girlfriend was pregnant. Although I felt sorry for her, I was finally free of him.

After years of bad relationships and major disappointments, I was left feeling emotionally beaten and no longer believing in true love. People weren't pure. I began to wonder why I was so unlucky in love.

My oldest brother once said, "You never dated anyone that deserved you." He told me that he believes I am gifted and have an amazing personality and don't even realize my own worth. Looking back at those relationships, there had to definitely be some sort of lack of self-worth.

Was God preparing me for something bigger? Each relationship *was* a lesson that brought me closer to my purpose. Whatever the reason, these were now my life lessons. Sometimes we need to hurt to grow mentally and spiritually, but I wondered how much more pain I would be able to bear.

Unfortunately, for many reasons, it took me much longer than the average person to learn my lessons. I kept repeating them before I start evolving.

For years, I decidedly remained single. I was very content and learned to love my own company. This is essential for every person out there. In order to truly love another, you must love yourself first. To attract kindred souls, you must first heal *yourself.*

My flaws are obvious, but one thing that remains constant and strong is my love. When shown love or appreciation, I return it tenfold. At the same time, when I feel crossed or disrespected, I will swiftly retaliate. My tolerance for injustice is little to none, but my ability to love is limitless.

I've become like an M&M candy with a hard shell and a soft interior. I have a very strong spirit, and even with all the disappointment and betrayal, I am *still* hopeful in love. I am just much more cautious and have a very low tolerance for BS. Life hardened me a bit too much—or maybe I just need to be softened to the woman who lives within the core of this hard shell.

Today, I live with very few regrets. I take everything as being fundamental in the development of my individuality and character.

These experiences have changed my beliefs about myself, my life, and the world. I needed them to grow and gain wisdom. I needed to break the beliefs that were instilled in me and create my own. Sometimes that process involves deep and painful lessons. Even though the sum of this pain landed me in a dark, depressive state, I still know it was all necessary.

I remind myself that there is always something worse; these were merely scratches that would eventually heal. They were possibly the consequence of having to raise myself, so to speak, living alone without emotional support or guidance for so long, including the result of a strict, sheltered upbringing that instilled a great deal of innocence and naivete.

Fall. Get up. Fall. Get up. Fall. Get up. Just keep getting up.

Live, learn, grow, and move on.

Chapter 6
Death and Loss

How do you feed a heart when it yearns for something you cannot give it? What do you do when it leaves a throbbing, burning pain in your chest from the hole that has been left there after the death of a loved one?

We all know that death is inevitable, but when you actually lose someone you love dearly, it can destroy you. You feel like a piece of you died and has left you asking questions you've never asked before. It takes your mind to places it has never gone; it brings a roller coaster of emotions, mystification, and new fears of the unknown.

Mom

I was only ten years old when I lost my mom in an accident, but from that moment on, my hopes of ever getting to really know her and have her as a part of my life were gone. Lord knows there were times that I desperately needed her unconditional love, support, and guidance.

When she died, I didn't understand death. I was too young to even understand life. It was my first experience with death, and at that age, things of that sort were way above anything I could comprehend or deal with. I didn't know how to react or feel. Instead, I lived in my mind, which was safe and easy.

Adults wonder why some children don't cry or react a certain way. Since it was above my comprehension, I tried to pretend it didn't happen. I kept on being a child, which is exactly how I felt at that age.

What is death? Where do people go when they die? Why do we die? Why do bad things happen?

To a child, the world is usually a fantasy land of fun, beauty, and magic. *What is this darkness?* I couldn't handle it. It was too scary.

I thought about her often, and I wished she were still here. I made certain that I wouldn't allow myself to forget the memories I did have with her before her death. I sometimes felt hollow growing up without my mother's love. I can't imagine having a constant source of love and support. I get annoyed when people are mean to their mothers, especially when they don't appreciate having them.

Her death deprived me of many mother-daughter moments. I still yearn for her. My heart still burns to feel it. Now as I write and think, it still burns.

The day of her funeral and burial played out like a movie in my mind. I recall it as if it were yesterday. It was such an awakening day. No one was smiling, playing, or laughing as a child was used to. People were sad, crying, and mourning. It was dark. It was like nothing I had ever experienced.

Being a visual person, I just covered my eyes and replayed that day in my mind. I can still see the entire scene, all these years later, and I still feel the stab of pain in my heart.

I walked into the funeral home with my head down, and I was afraid to look up because I didn't know what I was going to see. Also, there were a lot of people, and I was a shy child. As I walked in with my eyes directed to the floor, I passed many pairs of adult feet on both sides of me. I was stopped in the middle of the room in front of—unaware at the time—my mother's coffin.

My oldest sister let out a painful, heart-wrenching howl of a cry.

I was startled and looked up. There was a dead person in a coffin! I had never seen a dead person. It was my mom! I was so scared. My mom was *really* dead. I immediately covered my eyes. I couldn't cry. I couldn't do anything. I thought, *Please make this not be true! Get me out of here! I'm only a kid. Why would they make me see this? It's too scary!*

I will never forget that day. After what seemed like an eternity, standing there covering my eyes, I found the courage to take another quick glance at my mother. I knew it would be the last time I would ever see her. She was dressed in white and looked angelic. She had such a peaceful look on her face. I was so sad about losing her. I hope God took her home. She was a devout Catholic, and whenever I hear church bells, I still think of her.

We all drove to the cemetery for the burial. I'd never seen a casket being put into the ground. I didn't want insects touching my mom, and I thought there must be a more respectful way of handling dead people. Even at that age, I told myself that when I grew up, I would have her taken back to Europe, her birthplace. When I was an adult, her sister told me that my mother would have wanted to be where her children were and to leave her in peace.

This whole day was difficult. When I got home, I was afraid to sleep alone. Thankfully, I was allowed to sleep next to my middle brother who was my closest sibling. We were her two youngest children.

In the days that followed, I started to be a child again. I pretended that it was all a bad dream; that coping mechanism worked well. For several years, I pushed the images out of my mind and into a deep place within. I didn't mourn her death until the emotions flooded me at age twenty-one when an aunt who lived in Europe sent me pictures of her of when she was young. It's strange how long it took me to deal with repressed emotions and finally mourn my mother. During those eleven years, I did not visit her grave. Finally, at age twenty-one and in an arranged marriage, I felt ready to face those memories again. I was ready to speak to her, and I purchased a ticket and boarded a plane from New York City to do just that.

On a sunny and clear September day, my middle sister drove me to the cemetery. It was very large, and many roads ran through different lots. It was serene, clean, and peaceful, and it had beautiful landscaping and healthy green grass. It was heavenly for a cemetery. I felt content that she was there. I didn't remember it from when I was there as a child, even though it was the first time I had ever been to a cemetery, I must have not been looking out of the window or was lost in a daze from the whole ordeal.

We drove around for a while until we finally found the lot she was buried at. We needed to search for her plot among dozens of others that were there. When I first stepped out of the car, I felt like I was moving in slow motion. I was overcome with emotions and flooded with flashbacks of the day of her burial when I was ten years old.

I wore all white that day since it reminded me of the last time I saw her and how angelic she looked. I felt sad, ashamed, and guilty that I hadn't had the courage to go sooner. I had a lot I wanted to share with her.

My sister was getting annoyed that she had difficulty finding the grave even though she had been there before. At first, I just stood there by the car to gather my emotions and thoughts. I relived the day of her burial and recalled the mental images to guide me. I started walking slowly—as if I were being directed—and I stopped almost directly in front of her grave. It was crazy. I felt numb as I read her headstone.

My sister saw me from afar and yelled, "Did you find it?"

I nodded, and she came over.

Weeds and grass were covering part of her name, but we quickly cleared it all away. I felt like she had been neglected. It hurt so badly. I felt like a loser and a terrible daughter. My heart pulled at me, and my eyes filled with tears. I thought about how pointless life is. *You die and become nothing—just a memory.* It was all very sad.

I asked my sister to leave me alone with my mother, and she kindly waited in the car. I spoke to my mom for a while and remembered feeling aggravated that I didn't know if she could even hear me or see the lady I have grown up to be. I didn't know what she thought of me or if she even knew about the miserable arranged marriage I was in. I hoped she didn't. I wondered if she was at peace. Was her soul sad? My heart started to burn, and I began to cry very hard. Not knowing was hard to deal with; I did not have peace in my heart about my mother.

This is tugging at my soul as I write. My eyes are burning, and I am crying. I had to pause to get a box of tissues to wipe away my tears. Reliving it opened my scars and brought me right back to those painful feelings. It will always hurt. Always.

I sometimes imagine what kind of person I would be today if she were still alive and had helped raise me. My life would have been much different—and probably less tormenting. I desperately needed her to help me become a woman, to guide me, to steer me clear of mistakes, to wipe my tears, to share my secrets and fears, to laugh with me, to be at my wedding, and to someday hold my children. Knowing that I—and she—will never have this hurts beyond words.

I was very fortunate to be raised by a wonderful stepmother who is a very nice woman and a great homemaker, but only your mother is your mother.

My Middle Brother—My Best Friend

When I was twenty-six years old, I got the worst phone call of my life. On December 26, a father lost his son, two children lost their father, and my brothers and sisters and I lost our loving brother in a cold-blooded murder. He had been in the wrong place at the wrong time.

We are a very tight-knit family, and his death completely destroyed us. Each member of our family is a piece of a puzzle that equals one heart. With one piece missing, the rest remain broken forever. Time has made us learn to accept his loss, but it has not healed the pain.

My brother was a God-loving man who was extremely kind, loving, loyal, generous, and compassionate. He was full of love and light, loved all people, was free-spirited, loved music, sang and wrote songs, and was hilariously funny. Bringing joy and laughter to others brought him great pleasure. He was especially sensitive to people who were suffering in any way, and he was known to often give of himself selflessly to help those in need in whatever way he could. If he only had five dollars in his pocket and you needed it, he would've given it to you without hesitation. That is the man he was. If you knew him, you would have easily become his friend too. He was not a man to be forgotten. We will forever continue to mourn the loss of such a great man.

He died on the day after Christmas, and as the world celebrates each year, for us, it is a reminder of that tragic day.

I think of my father and cannot imagine what it felt like for him to have to bury his own child. At the wake, I saw my stoic father's knee's cave in. His legs were unable to carry him, and he nearly collapsed at the side of his son's coffin when he attempted to say goodbye and ask for forgiveness as a parent. That painful moment is scorched in my mind, and I'm sure it will remain in our father's heart until the end of time.

My heart also breaks for my younger brother. I can't imagine the horrible, heart-wrenching feeling of having to identify his brother's body. His loyal best friend had been murdered. A part of him died in that moment—as did a part of all of us that day.

My late brother was a symbol of pure love, and a life lacking him is a life lacking love.

He was only twenty-seven years old. We were only a year and eleven months apart. Like twins, we grew up extremely close. He was my best friend. I still yearn for his presence in my life, his unconditional brotherly love, and his friendship. He was the only person in this world who I was able to confide in about anything without being judged. I continue to live with a hole in my heart since his death, and nothing can feed that empty space since there is no other person in this world who can take his place.

After more than two decades, I still look for my brother's face in the crowd.

It took his death for me to realize that he was the only person who loved me unconditionally. That was huge. I felt a great void in my life from that point on—and here come the waterworks and burning in my chest as I write this. That pain has never gone away.

Our family dynamics didn't make sense without his presence. Wherever he went, he graciously spread love and light to us and others. He loved love in all its facets; he was a beautiful soul. I have yet to meet anyone else like him. It was as if God gave us an angel to teach us about love. He came, touched our lives, and left his example of love. We were so lucky to have him even for as short a time as we did. All families need one of him. We had no idea how lucky we were until he was gone. I will never forget the love he showed me. His love was very unique. I miss him so much. I miss his hugs, and I miss his voice.

I was a ten-year-old child when my mom died, and I didn't know how to process that loss. Losing my brother at age twenty-six was extremely different. It was the first time I really mourned death. The tremendous emotional pain was accompanied by hallucinations. I couldn't accept his death. I was inconsolable. I was living alone in

New York—far from family—and I grieved completely alone. It was extremely difficult. I was completely lost.

Although we lived in different states, we were still very close. He would visit me, call me, and even write to me. I still have all the letters he wrote. The thought of not having him a phone call away was heartbreaking. Oftentimes, when life got too tough for him, he would call me to vent. We understood each other more than anyone else understood us. We were both pure and kind as young adults, and we had both been taken advantage of and hurt many times. We were not people who could deal with the unjust pains of life. It hurt us much deeper than the average person. We just wanted to laugh and smile all the time and pretend the world was more peaceful than it really was. We had a lot in common, and his death left me feeling extremely alone. I felt like half of me died with him—because it did.

A large piece of my being disappeared instantly. It was clear that he was a huge part of who I was. I felt a black hole, a void in my chest, when I lost him. I still feel that way, but I also feel that a part of him is alive in me. I changed. Sometimes I do or say certain funny things that were more like his personality than mine. I was more reserved, and he was just hysterical.

I became more like him in the years after his death. It's like I took on his personality and combined it with my own; it was a beautiful combination. I made no intentional effort to do that. It just happened naturally. There may have been something supernatural about it, but I have not been able to understand it yet.

His death also brought me great wisdom and hardened my reality. I used to coast through life like a fairy, and I believed in love and happiness on a fairytale level. Maybe it was because I couldn't live in the reality of the part of life that I saw as painful, cruel, and evil. However, after his murder, darkness and evil were all that I saw. I was living in a dark, painful, cruel existence, and I was terrified.

One night, I took a walk to a park in the pouring rain. I was drenched, hysterically crying, and feeling completely lost. I called out his name, fell to my knees in the mud, and tried to understand where he had gone and if he could hear me anymore. I felt like I was not a part of life anymore.

Another time, while I was driving on the Bronx River Parkway, I began to cry uncontrollably. The tears fell like a rainstorm, and I could not see the road ahead of me. I screamed out his name as I drove, and I yelled, "Where are you?"

I looked at my passenger seat and wondered if his soul was there next to me. That type of pain took me to another place mentally. I felt his presence in the passenger seat that night. I felt like he was sad to see me like that. I am sitting in Barnes & Noble as I write this, and tears are streaming down my face.

After his death, I battled such a great level of sadness, and the pain was overcoming my mind. I could not sleep for weeks. I started hallucinating about his dead body covered in blood lying next to me in bed. It was horrific. I was wide-awake, but I couldn't even control my thoughts or visions. It was a terribly lonely and haunting time. The few times I did finally pass out from exhaustion, I would have nightmares about his death. It all played out like a horror movie and felt so real. I woke up in panic and terror. I was terrified about falling asleep again.

I barely ate or drank for weeks, and I probably dried out my kidneys because I ended up in the emergency room twice within two weeks passing kidney stones. It was excruciating physical pain on top of my emotional pain.

The doctor stormed into my room after reviewing my blood work and asked, "Do you eat?" He told me that my bloodwork showed that I was malnourished, but it didn't faze me or concern me at all. All I wanted was my brother back.

To make matters worse, most of my friends completely disappeared when they heard I was in mourning. No one came to comfort me, be present, help me sleep, bring me something to eat, or offer an ear or a cup of coffee. Nothing. I was there for each of them whenever they needed me—and not only in good times. I guess I was naive to think that if you were a loyal, caring friend to someone that they would care for you just as much or at least half as much. And where was the man I loved and loyally waited for for almost a decade? The Scorpio later told me that he didn't know what to say to me because he felt bad. That's selfishness—not love. I was deeply disappointed in everyone.

I became aware of the harsh reality of life and the lack of goodness and reciprocation in people. It saddened me greatly. It was a rude awakening that we are truly alone in this world with just a few, if any, sincerely loving and loyal friends.

My brother was my only true friend, and now he was gone forever. I felt so abandoned, and my world became cold and lonely.

Mother Teresa said, "The most terrible poverty is loneliness and the feeling of being unloved."

Since the pain of my brother's death was clearly beyond me, for the first time in my life, I sought professional help. I went to see a clinical psychologist, and it was the first time I had ever shared my life's secrets with any other human being.

At first, I was very reluctant, but in time, I ended up talking about more than just the present pain from the loss of my brother. My therapist was stunned to hear about the life I had lived, and she was amazed by the strength I had and how I was able get a college degree, find a career, support myself, and have no addictions—all while being alone without any family nearby. She told me that many people who had endured even less than what I had at my age would have sought drugs or alcohol or taken the wrong moral path.

She said, "Although you have been to the cliff many times, you never jumped."

I had never thought about how strong I was until she made me realize it. I just kept hustling through life, school, and my career to survive. I didn't see any other way. Even so, she reassured me that I was stronger than I thought I was, and that strength would help me through the grieving process.

In matters of losing a loved one, I have learned to celebrate their life instead of mourning their death. It is important to cherish the memories you shared together, look at pictures or watch videos, relive cherished times, and fill your heart with love instead of sadness or grief. It hurt, but in time, I grew to focus on how grateful and lucky I was for the time we *did* have together. I also learned to cherish all of my current relationships. You never know when the last goodbye will take place—and age doesn't matter.

Love your loved ones—unconditionally—and let them know it often.

Chapter 7
Seeking Him

In order to follow my spiritual path through life, you must also understand my religious exposure—or lack of—in my youth, the beliefs that were instilled in me, and the lessons that life has taught me.

I was the child of parents of two different religions: Muslim father and Catholic mother. I never frequented a mosque or a church as a child. I was educated about God by my father in a more nondenominational manner, but we were considered Muslim and celebrated the holidays. Religion played no part in many of the traditions of our culture. They were separate.

As a teenager, I fasted for Ramadan—just as many Muslims did around the world. Giving up something for God was a good feeling. My father never made us do it. It was something I decided to experience on my own, and I felt honored to do it for God. My father was proud of me.

Islam is a peaceful religion. Ignore the hateful media images that are based on terrorism.

The differences between my parents' religions did not matter to me since only God mattered. I wish the world today shared this outlook. The exposure to both religions was beneficial to me since it did not embed any discrimination in me. It created a person without prejudice regarding the different paths to God. I love Jesus, and I love Muhammad. I respect both religions, but I never felt like I belonged to either faith.

When I was in college, I enrolled in a course on religious studies to try to see which, if any, I fit best with. However, I still never felt like I belonged to any particular one.

I spent most of my twenties not really thinking about God or who He was. I was young, unwise, and relishing in my youth. After my brother died, filled with grief and hopelessness, I was led to Him. I felt the need to connect. I started to pray to Him, talk to Him, and ask questions and favors. I created a direct relationship with Him—without religion.

Even though I had no religion, I still felt like I wanted a place to worship other than just my home. I found a quiet little chapel, and there was usually no one there when I went, which I liked because I felt like it was just Him and me. The chapel became the only place in the world that I felt safe and peaceful. Throughout the years, I left buckets of tears on its benches.

I Cannot Fly

My wings are heavy.
I cannot fly.
Though free-spirited I once was.

I have been bruised.
I need to heal.
My energy has been blocked.

I stay in solitude,
With only my thoughts.
Only God can hear me now.

As I sit and pray for others,
I then turn within.

There, I find a mass confusion.

I ask God for direction,
For my own has steered me wrong.
At the fork, I get lost once again.

The bigger picture I am trying to paint.
But my Faith is low and vision blurred.
So, I sit, lost, in the house of the Lord.

Only here I can exhale.
Only here I can feel peace.
Guide me, Lord, to find my way to your will.
Heal my wings so that I can fly once again.

On one of my frequent visits there, I stumbled on a small prayer book called *My Daily Bread* written by Anthony J. Paone, SJ, in 1954. It is simple to read, and I felt like God was directly speaking to me about any subject I was concerned with. I love the book. Although it is a Christian-based book, I feel like everyone should own one. It teaches so much and has brought me tremendous peace in times of need. I have bought several copies and sent it to various friends of mine as gifts.

I believe that no one should judge the faith or path of others since we are *all* sinners and equal. I also believe that we are each called to Him personally by the trials and tribulations He sends to our lives. There is no need to knock on doors or pressure people; we will go when we are ready, and it is Him who makes us ready.

Sadly, as loving and as peaceful as religion is meant to be, it has become a significant cause of hate, division, and war. The ego converts the teachings and seeks superiority—hence attempts to create it.

What makes one religion better than another? What makes a Christian better than a Muslim or vice versa? The ego.

God is love.

Although religion didn't seem to resonate personally with me, faith in God did. My relationship with Him is one with myself. This has always felt right to me. Some may call me an agnostic theist or a heathen, but I don't care about labels. I just am.

I believe that God is everywhere—with and within you. He may also come in any form: Jesus, Muhammad, or the homeless person asking you for money.

A higher power, your higher self, energy, universal consciousness, God within—or whatever you want to call it, in this book, I call this God.

At this point in my life, I conclude that God has no religion—and neither do I.

If you love God, I love you.

2005 Self-revelation: God doesn't punish people. They punish themselves by not living like Him.

This is a song that I wrote in 2010 (never yet composed).

Thank You, God.

On this night filled with silence, I am all alone.
Lost in my thoughts,
Only my tears befriend me.
This life, like war, I am trying to survive.
So much sorrow, so little happiness.

I pray to God not to forsake me during these trying times.
I promise to accept all struggles that He sends me.
Such is this earthly life,
Sometimes sun, sometimes rain,
Sometimes laughter, sometimes pain.

Dear Lord, Almighty God,
Life doesn't make sense without you.

While all else fails,
You are the only thing that is true.
Thank you. I love you.

2014 Letter to Myself

Times of darkness falls upon us during many different periods of our lives. It is during these times that we tend to seek God, and He makes us aware of his presence. When all else seems gone, lost, or hopeless, He is always present, forgiving, and loving. He is always there when it feels like no one else is. This is how faith is strengthened. You feel Him in your darkest hours. He is the little light and hope left inside of you that you need to focus on and illuminate once again. Focus on the light and not on the darkness that you have allowed to take over.

Through suffering, many of us are led to Him. Through suffering, He is revealed to many who otherwise take Him for granted. I have been guilty of this many times, but I am grateful for my struggles because they are the foundation of my growth and getting to know my Creator.

During many of my own life's most painful times, I have searched deeply within myself for peace, for Him. I searched in churches and mosques and made pilgrimages to holy sites such as Medjugorje, Croatia. I have traveled to Spain, Brazil, and even South Korea. It took several years to realize that I did not need to go anywhere for God. Peace is within me. It was me who needed to bring Him—that Light—to the surface and be present in my life. Several years and bouts of depression have brought me a rich spiritual life.

In 2005, I made a promise to God that I would never love anyone or anything more than Him. Only then will I never feel alone. Through severe depression, I found God—and He made me aware that true love and peace only exist through Him.

I am crying as I write this. I am ashamed because I have fallen off this wagon many times. I have to remind myself that we are only weak human beings who are constantly influenced by earthly challenges and desires.

Chapter 8

I, the Artist

I started writing and singing at about age ten or eleven. I would memorize every word to many ethnic songs that my father would listen to and perform them in front of an invisible audience at first. These were songs from my cultural background since that was what I was exposed to most. My late brother also had a strong desire for music and singing, so we would start performing together whenever we had company. We were not shy at all in that aspect. The stage always felt like my true playground. The world was his.

Being raised in a strict family where the girls were brought up to become good housewives, not performers, I never imagined I would ever become a singer. I just viewed it as a hobby that would never become real.

After my brother passed away, singing and performing became my therapeutic release and the only thing that brought me happiness and healing.

The day after his death, I sat in isolation in a back bedroom at my parents' house. I wrote a heartfelt poem for him while the rest of my family sat together mourning. I had lived alone in New York for some time, and I was used to dealing with things in solitude.

A few years later, I took a folder full of poems and songs I had written over the years to a well-known composer in New York. He was from the same cultural background, and I told him that I was not a professional singer, but I wanted to make a CD in honor of my late brother. At that point in my life, that was all I wanted. Nothing else. I wanted to honor him and his greatness in our lives. Later, the poem I wrote the day after his death in that back bedroom was composed into a song, along with my first CD, which I dedicated to him.

The CD was complete within a few months. The day I received the final copy was the happiest day of my life. If I had died at that moment, I would have died truly happy. It was a magnificent, heartfelt tribute to the most beautiful human being, and we had loved each other unconditionally. I accomplished what I wanted, and my brother lived on through me. The people who did not know him then knew of him now; my amazing brother always encouraged me to sing because he knew I loved it.

I absolutely loved every second of the entire experience of making that CD—the singing, the songwriting, expressing myself, and spending time at the studio—but I never had any intention of becoming a singer. It wouldn't be accepted.

Unexpectedly, the making of that song and my CD opened the door to other connections. The composer introduced me to a musician who was taking piano lessons with him since he wanted to be a part of a band as the keyboard player. Both inexperienced, we started practicing together. We rehearsed in a studio, and before we knew it, we started performing at small gigs. This started my journey into the music world: the forbidden world to my family. It was the world of pure happiness for my soul.

The musician and I started working in all types of cultural bars and lounges to get the experience we desired. Although I started singing and performing out of sheer love and happiness, it also proved to be quite lucrative. This went on every single weekend for more than a decade while I maintained a full-time job.

Looking back, how did I do that? Where did I get all of that energy? I was like Superwoman. Music didn't feel like work, but it did consist of several hours of standing and singing until about four o'clock in the morning. I looked forward to the weekends so much because it was so fun and made me so happy. I couldn't imagine living without that electrifying feeling. I had never felt so happy or alive in my entire life.

For the first few years, I didn't tell my family because I knew it was unacceptable and considered disgraceful to have their daughter be a performer of any sort, especially in places like social clubs where mostly men hung out. However, I wasn't there for them; I was there for my soul. Nothing made me happier, and my need for it superseded my family's disapproval. When they found out, I was told to quit. I told them that they might as well tell me to stop smiling! It was my only true love, and it guaranteed happiness when life and human love had failed me. It was my only constant and unfailing joy. I needed them to understand that. I would not give it up for anything.

While I am singing, there is a point where I become one with the music. There is a floating feeling that brings complete and utter bliss. I feel completely euphoric. I feel a high of satisfaction that life alone seldom brings. It makes me live in the moment. I am completely consumed by inner joy. It is a place of zero stress. There are no problems and no depression. Nothing. Just ecstasy. It was so great that it also superseded making marriage or having a family a priority even in my thirties.

I was a fireball of energy and light. I was very social and outgoing—a far cry from the seventeen-year-old shy virgin bride who waddled for the first time in heels through the airport in a wedding dress more than a decade ago. I was told by a professional singer that I naturally had a charming and captivating presence and was meant to be on stage and made so much money naturally—without putting in much effort. He told me it was clear to the customers that I was different, not greedy or desperate, which made me more appealing to them and deserving of their tips.

I am an artist, not just a singer, and I perform for the love of the art and not the love of the dollar bill. This can only attract positivity. Making money by doing something you love was a bonus.

It was a hobby that turned into a second job. Performing at gigs became my drug of choice for years. If there was to be any addiction, that was mine. It was a release of any pent-up emotions or pain. It brought so much happiness, therapy, and joy that I hardly even realized just how lucrative it was. It was priceless therapy.

These were the happiest years of my life. When I think about myself during that time, the first thing that comes to mind is my constant smiling face.

The Tainting of My Bliss

My love for music and the need for the therapy it provided kept me returning every single weekend for close to fifteen years. Although I also performed at some weddings and other family-oriented events, the majority of my gigs were in members-only clubs frequented by men and infested with cigarette smoke and alcohol. If it weren't for my love of music, I would have never hung out there.

For many years, I was lost in the music and ignored the harsh reality that there was little to no appreciation for the art; as it was, more so than not, a bunch of intoxicated men gawking at the singer. As the years went by, I felt sad as I drove home after gigs. I felt like I was selling myself and not like the artist or the self-respecting woman I was.

The gigs started getting worse throughout the years because certain singers I occasionally worked with started behaving degradingly to make extra money. Some would get up on tables while singing when asked by intoxicated or low-class customers. This consequently taught customers that it was okay for them to treat singers disrespectfully. It was pathetic and disgusting. I was sick to my stomach about being in the same room as these women and watching that behavior. It created problems for me when customers had the nerve to ask me to do the same thing and I refused. I told one guy that I would give him double the money to never ask me that again. I wanted to break his teeth for insulting me.

My happy spot was tainted. Class was dead. The beauty of the art was ruined. It was more like entertainment for desperate men. I didn't want to be there, and I did not want that dirty money. My dignity was not for sale.

Some customers came up to me and said, "You are too good for this place. Why are you here?"

I realized it was time for a change of scenery. That part of my life had to be greatly minimized; I became very selective about where I chose to work and with whom I would work. I had grown and evolved spiritually. I needed a new, more positive outlet that would benefit the world—and not just me anymore.

I started researching ways to extend myself musically and otherwise. I started getting back into my writing, which I've always loved, and I also started taking guitar lessons. I hope to someday use my talents to perform for the less fortunate, especially children.

Chapter 9
Ugly Me

Since my loyalty in friendships and romantic relationships had often been betrayed and/or taken advantage of, I grew bitter in life and was easily angered. The world appeared evil, and I grew intolerant and inpatient to any level of what I considered bullshit.

I became very short-tempered, confrontational, and defensive. I was nothing like the girl who came to New York several years prior. I wasn't one to start problems, but if someone attacked me in any way, they would feel my wrath. I also became sharp with my tongue and would easily cut people out of my life. I could be outright cold, ruthless, and hurtful when I was crossed or betrayed or felt any injustice being done to me. Otherwise, when people were kind, I was ten times as kind.

On that note, I recall an embarrassing thing I did several years ago. It was fueled by anger. I contemplated whether I wanted to share it since it was a really ugly part of who I had become, but I must keep the promise I made when I decided to write this book and share it. It is also important to see the level of pain I was carrying, which turned into the ugly face of anger.

Please don't hate me. I am no longer her.

***

One summer afternoon, as I was driving home and proceeding to get off the highway into the single-lane exit, out of nowhere, a man aggressively accelerated to pass me and cut me off. It completely startled me and nearly caused me to hit the fence as he ran me off the road. My temperature instantly rose, and I immediately felt overcome with anger.

A few feet ahead of me, he was stopped at a red light. I caught up to him and was behind his car. Without thinking twice—or at all—I got out of my car, went up to his window, and cursed him out.

Instead of apologizing or showing any remorse, he condescendingly laughed at me.

My temper turned from anger to rage, and I punched him as he sat in his car.

Apparently shocked, he grabbed my arm in an attempt to stop me, which left many scratches.

When I came out of my oblivion, I realized that I was being observed by motorists all around us. I must have looked like a madwoman. I was so embarrassed and ashamed of my behavior. I snapped out of my moment of insanity, rushed back to my car, and quickly drove away.

In that moment of anger, it felt good to knock the lights out of that arrogant asshole, but as I drove away, I reflected on my behavior and realized I was no better than he was. I began to cry in sadness and shame, concerned with who I had become.

The pain and disappointments of my life were boiling over. I was angry and resentful because I had never treated people poorly, taken advantage of them, or betrayed anyone. Injustice of any kind became my trigger.

I started to hate who I was becoming, and I wanted to do whatever it took to go back to normal. People who knew me during that time described me as a nice and kind girl—but one not to fuck with because I was the extreme opposite when I was angry.

I was an angel or a devil, depending on which buttons you pressed. There was no in-between.

I released my anger by giving it back tenfold to feel better since it had been undeservingly inflicted upon me. It was fed by its own ugly source. It was dangerous. I had to kill it. It got worse every year, and I sunk into depression. I was losing my true identity, which saddened me greatly.

Chapter 10
The Fall

Letters to God

"Dear God, What are you trying to show me? I have felt the pains of life. The pain of betrayal, of love, of hunger for emotional fulfillment, of abandonment and rejection. I have felt pain physically, emotionally, and mentally—to the point of complete exhaustion. I have suffered through times of hopelessness, despair, grief, and extreme loneliness. I have bled internally from pain greater than what I ever imagined I could endure. I have been to the cliff many times, but I somehow succeeded in not jumping off. I have been hit by tragedies and crises that many people do not experience during their lifetimes. Completely alone, I have suffered and endured all these times. At times, I felt my soul eating at itself.

Just when I survived these difficult periods and regained my strength, I was knocked back down by another. If this has all been a test to strengthen me, I should now be made of stone. If this has all been a test of character, then I feel like I am failing. Roughness and arrogance have taken the place of the sweetness and innocence I once owned.

These trials and tribulations have built my character and created the person I am today. My heart has hardened. My spirit has been scarred. Unhappy is my state of mind. Maybe it will all make sense someday, but right now, it's weighing down on my soul. It has put me in a state of depression."

I was built like a rock. I had the ability to sustain any storm or obstacle and clearly move past it. I had an unstoppable and infallible character by nature, and I was a master at climbing in life. Family, friends, and people who knew me often told me that they admired my perseverance and strength. However, truth be told, I never saw or thought about it unless someone mentioned it to me. I was just surviving.

I endured my falls and heartbreaks completely alone, and I never shared them with my family. I didn't want to share any of my failures—funny how I saw them as failures instead of lessons—and I didn't want to give them any of my headaches. I chose to live alone. I would make it alone. My family was still very culturally driven, but I no longer was. I couldn't expect support as a free-thinking woman who was living in what was considered a culturally unacceptable lifestyle. I kept almost all of my private life private. No one was there to pick me up but myself—every time. It seemed doable since it was my norm … until it wasn't.

That was the price for my freedom, and because I needed it desperately and desired nothing more, I *had* to take my falls alone. I wouldn't have grown into who I am without it. For almost three decades, I bottled everything inside—until, eventually, I erupted like a volcano.

***

Some of the funniest people in the world are also some of the saddest people in the world. It reminds me of Robin Williams, the late comedian and actor, and his longtime battle with depression. Ironically, humor and making others happy was his strength, but he couldn't make himself happy. I *completely* understand that and empathize with him.

A friend of mine once told me that I was "accidentally funny" because I was funny even when I didn't try to be. I've always craved humor, and it came naturally. To me, where there is humor, there is peace. Humor also made me temporarily forget about my own issues, and it provided an escape from the grim reality and darkness in the world. I've always wanted to be around funny, easygoing people, and I love creating the ambience of peace through humor.

My family, friends, and coworkers gravitated toward my bubbly and fun-loving personality—or so I was told—knowing there would always be laughter and fun around me. Sometimes I would do or say something, and I'd be the first one to laugh at myself and how funny it was. I didn't know where it came from, but "Funny Me" was really entertaining, creative, and fun to be around. I loved when she was alive.

There were many years, even during my toughest times, where no one could tell that I was suffering and going through so much. I was so incredibly strong, and no matter how many times I was knocked down in life, I always got back up. I saw everything as temporary, and I didn't allow it to own me for too long. It might take several weeks, but I always put my happy face right back on and moved on. I was the one who appeared to always have her life in order. I had the ability to focus on fun, jokes, and laughter—no matter what turmoil laid beneath.

Yet, after over twenty years of very difficult trials and extreme bouts of loneliness, I began to break down. I literally could not be funny anymore or even pretend to be. I was cracking, and I couldn't even fake a smile. My soul hurt. New scars and the opening of previous ones started to bleed all at once. I went from laughter to pain. The eruption had begun.

***

How much can you hold in before erupting or breaking?

The sadness became the heaviest element within, and it exposed itself to the surface. It conquered me. You can't be funny when you are crying inside. It was too raw. My scars were bleeding. My demise was obvious to anyone who knew me. I was tired of being strong. I was too weak to pretend. My strength was gone. For the first time, I finally surrendered to my sorrow. It was too heavy to defeat. It was bigger than me.

To make matters worse, the negativity and bitterness in my new personality caused an alienation from all of my closest friends, leaving me alone with my sorrow. I was miserable and angry all the time. I was nagging, critical, confrontational, complaining, impatient, and intolerant. I never smiled, and I stopped being funny. My jokes turned into insults and nasty sarcasm.

I became the type of person I always avoided having anywhere near my inner circle. No one wanted to be around me anymore, and I didn't blame them. They missed the old me—and so did I. I didn't know how to be her again. All I felt was pain and hatred for my life. There was zero energy in attempting her awakening. Funny Me was now dead. I fell into a deep, dark depression that now owned me.

Depression

An estimated 350 million people worldwide are suffering from depression, and more than eight hundred thousand people commit suicide every year. Suicide is the second leading cause of death for fifteen-to-twenty-nine year-olds.[1] Many, many more people attempt suicide, and millions of people are affected by it. It destroys families.

---

[1] https://www.who.int/news-room/fact-sheets/detail/depression.

I will now provide a full, detailed, firsthand understanding of what it's like to go from mentally healthy to mentally ill. This is depression explained from its source.

***

Because of years of repeated episodes of disappointment, heartbreak, and emotional torment, I felt defeated. I became one of the many victims of depression. Every level of my core was too tired to be strong anymore. Stoic Me was also now dead. I was battered, beaten, and broken. My body felt lethargic, and getting out of bed in the morning was extremely difficult. I couldn't continue to fight my demons. I had absolutely no desire or energy to get up, get dressed, or go anywhere. I felt paralyzed by my mental state.

I was haunted by thoughts of my past misfortunes and increased feelings of hopelessness. I had been through too many failures, and they took a toll on my wounded heart and mind. I was defeated mentally, emotionally, and physically.

It is a great distraction to constantly live in your thoughts—your mind world—instead of just living in the moment. However, when you're suffering from depression, it is almost impossible to control. This is what people don't understand. Heaven and hell both exist in the mind. It is not a physical place. My mind became poisoned, and it felt like I was living in pure hell. Nothing made me happy. I couldn't even sing or listen to music anymore.

At that point, I had been dead for almost two years. I was like a flickering light bulb that was ready to die at any moment, but I could not wait for the flicker to finally go out. I wanted to end the pain.

Life was not something I wanted to be a part of anymore, and it felt impossible to ever be revived since I felt no hope or desire to live. A life without hope is like a flower without water, withering to a slow but imminent death.

In depression, you feel no hope or purpose for your existence. You feel like a waste of space and air. Imagine living with no hope and not having anything to look forward to. If you can't, you're lucky.

You can have a great job, loving relatives, and many blessings, but you feel so painfully unhappy. All the money in the world can't take away the pain or restore hope; this is proven by the suicides of wealthy people such as Kate Spade, Anthony Bourdain, and many, many more.

I had never been to such a dark place. Nothing had a point—not waking up, not working, not family, not friends, and not traveling. Absolutely nothing made me happy because it hurt to be alive.

There is a paralysis of your soul that takes place when you are stuck in such a dark place. It eats at you on so many levels. I had many long periods of solitude and detachment from everyone. Many times, it felt like the walls of my apartment were caving in on me. I went through stages of weeks and months of sleeping through entire days and/or weekends because dreaming was easier than facing reality.

Unfortunately, many people just don't understand this and label the sufferers selfish or weak. They think you can somehow magically just flip a switch and snap out of it, but you cannot. It is not that simple. It's not about control at all. You reach a point where you don't have an ounce of control left. You *cannot* control how you feel. *You feel paralyzed*.

It does not matter what is right or wrong when it's not what you actually *feel*. The feeling of pain cuts so deep and hurts so much that nothing can take it away—except death.

Many classify suicide as a selfish act. In the mind of the sufferer, it is *not* a selfish act at all. It is viewed as the best solution to all involved—whether anyone agrees with it or not. I am not encouraging it by any means whatsoever. I only ask that people become more knowledgeable, sympathetic, and understanding about what goes on in the thought processes of the sufferers.

It's upsetting when people who haven't actually lived in that hell world speak of it or judge its victims with shallow opinions and label them as selfish. In reality, they have no clue as to what they are talking about. Unless you have experienced it, you truly cannot imagine the complexity of it. It is not just black or white. Your soul has been taken over. It is a debilitating disease. Have sympathy for its victims. This isn't a subject you can make assumptions about.

Also, do not confuse it with a victim mentality. A victim mentality is where a person seeks attention, blames others, or wants people to feel sorry for them. On the contrary, I seldom—if ever—shared any of my experiences. I preferred to suffer in solitude. The last thing I wanted to endure was bringing more attention to my pain. And sufferers who consider suicide want people to stop feeling sorry for them and to stop feeling sorry for themselves. Be careful not to mislabel or minimize this illness as something that it's not.

At my breaking point, my family members became very worried. They noticed my drastic change and deterioration. I was always slim, but I lost a significant amount of weight and looked skeletal. I cried often for no apparent reason; the pain inside was too great. I didn't want to hurt them by sharing my suffering, but I literally could not hide it. It was evident that I wasn't the person they knew before.

I needed them to know that I wanted *out,* and if something happened to me, that I was okay with it. I called my father and said, "I don't belong to this life."

The phone went silent, and when he finally spoke, he said, "That is a terrible thing for a parent to hear from his child." He tried to give me encouraging words to strengthen my spirit, and he reminded me that it was just a temporary struggle. *This* was not me. I was so strong and positive, and I should shoot all the negative thoughts out of my mind. He reassured me that I wasn't alone.

***

A few years ago, my father told me that he felt guilty about my life because of the arranged marriage. He felt it was all his fault that I hadn't had any luck in finding a successful partner because of it, but I don't see things that way. A partner should complement you—not fulfill you—and I surely don't blame him for continuing the traditions that he was schooled in.

While raising six children, he learned so much about what he could have done differently—just as many other parents have. I blame him for nothing. It is also very important to share that I take full responsibility for everything that has happened to me in my life. I do not blame anyone. I am the master of my own world—just as everyone else is the master of theirs.

***

I still don't believe that my family knew exactly how badly I was suffering because they knew me as a survivor. They thought I was just going through a very rough patch and would get through it. However, this was very different. I was on the edge, and I desperately wanted to jump.

I recall when my father called to check in on me, and the moment I heard his voice, my voice cracked. I couldn't speak, and I instantly began to cry. I was in so much emotional pain, and I felt terrible about unintentionally causing him grief, especially at his age. He was in his late seventies. It hurt me to hurt my loved ones. (I am crying as I write this). I could no longer pretend to be okay. I just couldn't. I was in such great emotional pain. I was extremely sensitive. I was defeated. I knew I would never be the person I once was.

During that period, my father and siblings were very supportive. They checked up on me often and tried to give me strength. I am eternally grateful for my family and our bond. Their love, support, and concern helped me greatly, but at the time, I didn't realize it because I just wanted to be left alone to die. I didn't want attention. I only wanted the pain to be gone.

My father became my best friend when being a father wasn't enough. I don't know how I could have made it without my family.

I feel very grateful for having them, but it makes me feel sad for all the people in the world who don't have anyone during such times.

If you know of someone who is suffering from depression, you can help in even the smallest way by being present and being gentle. It can save their life. Do not judge or criticize. You never know how close to the cliff they are. They are already carrying too much pain. A cliff can seem like a solution to their agony.

Desiring Death: Letters to God

On New Year's Eve of 2014, I was home, painfully alone in the living room. All the lights were out except for a dim light of Mother Teresa, which is always on, and the many candles I had lit. It looked like I was in a sanctuary, which was the feeling I wanted to create. I wanted to be alone with God. My soul felt broken, and I desperately needed to talk to Him one-on-one.

Just before midnight, I knelt on my living room floor, faced all of the lit candles, and began speaking to Him. I recorded it all, and this is what I said to Him:

Dear Father,

I am at a lifetime low in my life. I don't want to hurt my family and have thought to call and ask them to forgive me, but I want to die. It would be easier to just die and make it stop forever. I will not hurt myself or anyone anymore.

Life itself seems to have no point: pointless and purposeless. Live, struggle, suffer, and then die. Why even be born? Being born is a punishment. It's almost cruel to do to a child.

Then I think if a person *truly* believes in God, he should never feel any lack of love, but I do. It's 11:34 p.m., almost 2014, and these are my feelings:

101

2013 and the rest of my past life have kicked my ass and stolen my innocence, my hope, and any desire to live. I have no dreams. Instead, my New Year's wish is only to die. I beg you to *please* just let me die.

I am truly exhausted of being a part of this struggle called life. I am completely burned—mentally, emotionally, and physically.

Am I carrying a cross to end someone else's suffering other than just my own? If so, I will continue to do so. I just need to know that I am suffering for a purpose.

Please show me, Father. It hurts to live.

God, I surrender to you. Do as you wish with me.

***

I was at the brink, and the pain was a constant fire burning in my soul. I desperately wanted it to stop. Living hurt. At that point, life and death were the same—except death would have been better since the pain would go away. I saw it as my savior. People who do not understand depression and/or suicide need to realize that *this* is the feeling of one who suffers from it.

Several years before my fall, the subject of suicide came up with some friends. I told them that if I were ever found dead that it would never be a suicide because I could never do something like that. At the time, I was speaking from ignorance. I assumed. I never imagined I would have this story to tell. This proves that even the strongest among us can break.

Many sufferers hide it from the public eye, leaving you in shock with the news of their suicide because they "seemed happy." In reality, we were constantly fighting mental demons. You feel like a *complete* failure to God, to yourself, and to those you love the most. It was bad enough that I couldn't control my own sadness, but I was also unintentionally hurting my loved ones. That was an additional heavy burden on my mental state. It was too heavy a cross for me to carry. I only wanted to disappear.

I thought, *As long as I'm alive and in this state of being, I will continually hurt my loved ones. Whereas, if I were dead, my pain would end—and their mourning will eventually subside.* Whether that sounds rational or not does not matter because when you are hurting every second of the day, the pain is too great to acknowledge anything less than it! Please read that again until you thoroughly understand it.

Even the grief that your family will feel after your death does not compare to the constant unbearable pain of living in it. Your soul feels like it has been set on fire. Do you think you would think about anyone else's feelings if you felt that level of excruciating pain and internal torture every moment of every day? No! You literally cannot. It must be stopped. That is all you can think. It hurts more than physical pain, which eventually goes away. The pain exceeds everything—even rationalization—and that is what leads many people to suicide.

To more fully understand, imagine loyal Christians who have committed suicide. Even knowing the Bible has taught them that they will not be allowed to go to heaven and will suffer an eternal burning hell for such an act, they *still* chose death by suicide. Death was heaven—no matter where it took them—even hell could not be worse than their pain. *That* might give you an idea of the level of pain they felt.

People who die by suicide don't do it to end their lives; they do it to end their pain.

My personal description of depression is this: It's like your soul is literally on fire. You want to scream in agony, but you are not allowed to make any audible sounds. It's terrible torture.

Chapter 11

Overcoming Depression

Many things are not medically proven, and as such, they should also not be dismissed. I believe in the mental and physical manifestation of disease from high stress in one's life and have watched it happen to me and many others. Through my years of working in the medical field, I was often told by patients that their cancer came during very trying times of their lives.

At the peak of my depressive state, I had manifested illness in the form of heart issues. A few years before, during a routine physical, I became aware of an irregular heartbeat. I was told it was common, and it was nothing to worry about. However, in my depressive state, I started suffering from anxiety and continual palpitations in my chest. It's a feeling of being very frightened for no apparent reason—an unexpected onset that went on several times a day for several months. It was uncomfortable and made it difficult to function and maintain a job in this condition, but I had no choice.

Finally, one night, as I lay in bed ready to go to sleep, I had a very scary and dangerous occurrence. My heart started pounding out of my chest; the heartbeats were very loud, thumping, and palpable. It was very unusual and unfamiliar. It went on uncontrollably and irregularly for several minutes. It consisted of several normal heartbeats followed by a few very loud, pounding ones. It felt like my heart was going to protrude out of my chest cavity.

This sequence went on for several minutes. It was a first-time occurrence for me, and it was obvious something was very wrong. I believed I was having a stress-related heart attack, but because of my depression, it didn't faze or frighten me. I didn't go to the ER. I thought, *This is how I will die. My suffering will finally end tonight.* I listened to it for a while until I allowed myself to fall asleep and accept my fate.

When I woke up back to normal the next day, I saw a cardiologist who worked in the same building as I did. Otherwise, I probably wouldn't have bothered. I didn't fear death. I feared dying in pain.

When I told the doctor what I had experienced, his eyes popped open. He told me that he couldn't believe I ignored it and just went to sleep. If it happened again, he told me to rush to the ER. He immediately had tests done on me and hooked me up to a heart monitor, which showed more than thirteen thousand irregular heartbeats in a twenty-four-hour period.

I asked, "What's a normal number?" He looked me sternly in the eye and responded, "About a handful." He tried to educate me about the significance of my health problem and get me to take it more seriously. He put me on medication, told me to see an electrophysiologist (who recommended an ablation), and gave me a fourteen-day heart monitor to check for progress. I was more annoyed than anything.

When I returned for my follow-up appointment, it was still too high at nine thousand beats per twenty-four hours. To me, it was a clear sign that the mind controls the body. I had clearly made myself physically ill.

Searching for the Light

After about two years of darkness, I was fucking fed up with always feeling sad—and I was now sick too. *I thought, If I'm not going to die, then I need to figure out how to live. I need to take at least one step forward. I desperately need a radical change.* This is very important advice for depression sufferers!

I was convinced that I needed to mentally make myself healthy, and that would be the only medication I required. I wasn't on any antidepressants or medications during that time. I didn't think masking it with meds would heal me or stop the pain. To be clear, I do not discourage it just because I felt that way at the time. I tried antidepressants for the first time after the loss of my brother, and it may have helped, but I was too sad to notice. I experienced brain zaps when I got off of them, which discouraged me from trying them again.

Against my doctor's orders, I decided to quit the heart meds. However, I did follow his advice to join a gym to strengthen my heart muscles and release endorphins for my mind. It was a double positive. It was an obvious benefit that I could no longer avoid if I had to be a part of the world. It also helped that the gym was right next door to my job. Since I couldn't avoid passing it every day, I stuck with it.

For the first several weeks, I had a very difficult time. I had never trained before. After weeks of reluctance—but persistence—I began to feel better after I left the gym. To my surprise, I even started to crave the burn from my workouts. I made friends with the trainers and felt like I was going to hang out with friends and not just work out. I was being social again, which I hadn't been in so long. I felt like a tiny flower trying to come out of the soil to sprout.

Working out should be accompanied by healthy eating; otherwise, you won't really see results. Diet has been proven to have a direct link to mental health and not just physical health. I changed my diet and significantly decreased my carb intake, and I started feeling good about how I looked and felt. In a few months, I begin to see improvement mentally as well as physically. I still felt sad—but not as often and not as much as I had in the past. I was now occupying my time in a positive manner. There was slow but obvious progress. I was clearly on the right path.

As Lao Tzu said, "A journey of a thousand miles begins with a single step."

The Power of the Mind

My nephew was paralyzed in a motorcycle accident at the age of nineteen and had been a paraplegic for several years. He said, "I never feel depressed."

I couldn't even begin to fathom that healthy state of mind, especially in his condition. I saw his daily struggles just to get dressed and get out the house. Instead of feeling defeated, he made it his new way of life.

My nephew deals with so much more than the average person does every single day, yet he can say and feel that he is never depressed. He is such a symbol of strength and courage, and he is a perfect example of the power of the mind. I thought, *Why can't I feel as positive as he does? Why do some people sink when others swim?*

I was always a swimmer—until I wasn't.

Chapter 12
Healing with Meditation

Prior to joining the gym, I decided to start practicing meditation. My mind was still consumed with thoughts that were robbing my life of peace. I was desperate for clarity and positive change. The person I had become, swallowed in sadness, was not me. For several years, I tried to find ways to be happy again. I tried everything I could think of—antidepressants, acupuncture, ayahuasca, pilgrimages to holy sites, therapy, psychics, and spiritual healers—but nothing helped. I was *still* unhappy. I didn't have God in my life during that time.

A friend handed me a pamphlet from a local meditation center. I learned that it reduces stress and can overcome depression. Meditation helps people find happiness and peace, become one with God/the universe, and ultimately find their purpose in life. Desperate for change, I ended up at the door of the center. I was assured that I would find healing through meditation—the silencing of the mind—and I gave it a try.

Several times in the first couple of months, I would drive there after work and park my car out front, but be physically unable to go inside. Instead, I'd fall asleep in the car, wake up later, and drive home. My depression made me emotionally exhausted and physically weak.

When I finally started going inside, I was extremely resistant and impatient. I complained constantly. I was skeptical and stubborn, and I did not like having to sit on a cushion on the floor for long periods of time, which was required to meditate. It was uncomfortable and irritating. They explained to me that the ego was creating this resistance, and they kept encouraging me to look passed it.

Many times, when I became too uncomfortable sitting, I slouched down onto the floor and fell asleep immediately. The meditation guides would wake me up and tell me that I had to sit up in order for it to be most beneficial. I huffed and puffed like a spoiled child, but I did as they asked. I was the most reluctant and difficult student. I don't know how they tolerated me and my nasty attitude. They were very kind, patient, and gentle.

For the first few months, I constantly fell asleep during class. Strangely, falling asleep during meditation was the best, most peaceful sleep I had ever experienced—even if it were only for a few minutes. Although I didn't see obvious results for months, I didn't quit since it was such a warm and caring environment. I made a lot of new and true friends there; they were all struggling in their own ways. Everyone is battling something. We all progressed together. It was like we were building a new family; we were all seeking peace.

After *much* resistance, in the months that followed, I very slowly began to surrender. *Surrender* is the key word in meditation. Even if I wanted to quit, I had nowhere else to go. I felt like I was not healthy enough to be a part of society. I would go straight there after work. I spent four or five nights there per week—two to five hours a night—for almost four years! I sacrificed my personal life, time with friends, dating, and anything fun or leisurely. My healing was my priority. I felt like the sacrifices were absolutely necessary. I was desperate in my quest for healing. I gained a lot of clarity—and in more ways than I ever imagined.

The helpers/guides who lived at the center were extremely peaceful, soft-spoken, compassionate, and understanding. They greeted their students with warm, welcoming smiles and hugs, if we needed them. They made food for us each night if we stayed past dinnertime. The students and guides would have dinner together during a short break between sessions and then return to the meditation room for another session. They created a family atmosphere.

Being at the center was better than going home to myself. I am very grateful to them for putting up with me in such a generous, loving, and compassionate manner. When I cried, they listened. They only spoke kind, encouraging words. They taught me so much. The stubborn mule in me softened and became more grateful.

The founder of the meditation center spoke little English, but he would continually say, "Patience." That was the element I lacked the most, but luckily, I had enough discipline to continue.

During meditation, we sat on the floor in a silent room, with cell phones off, guided by the helpers. As you get deeper and deeper into your mind, you see all the thoughts and pictures that come up. It was clear to see that my mind was flooded with so many images and thoughts, many of which proved useless and damaging to me. Painful memories often flashed before me and brought tears to my eyes. Tissues were always available.

Things that I wasn't aware of that were bothering me came to the surface. Even memories of things I thought I had completely forgotten or hadn't thought of since childhood. Within weeks, I started to clearly see the multitude of distractions that were controlling my mind. There were so many useless attachments and so much garbage. Meditation taught me to destroy them and clear my mind.

A Meditation Trip to South Korea

Within the first year of joining the meditation center, I decided to make a trip to the main center in South Korea. They offered intense courses to expedite progress. Desperate, I booked a trip there for twenty-one days. During this time, you had to abide to the strict rules of the center. I thought, *No problem. I'm ready.* However, time proved otherwise. It was not the meditation center in New York that I was used to.

Some of the more basic rules were no cell phone use, no television, no internet, and no male-female *bonding*—or any other bonding for that matter. Otherwise, you were kicked out of the center. There were cameras throughout the property to enforce the rules.

Going to the main center meant being in a large meditation room with several dozen other people from different parts of the world in intense meditation for twelve or thirteen hours per day! The whole time, we were expected to sit up straight on a cushion on the floor. Many people were able to do this, but I wasn't very flexible. It was not easy for me, and my back hurt every day. I was very uncomfortable and needed to change positions frequently.

Sleeping was not allowed during class, and if you fell asleep, which I did many times, one of the guides woke you up. Class began at eight thirty in the morning, and we were given a few short breaks during the day, plus a lunch and dinner break, and we resumed class until midnight. The cycle repeated again at eight thirty the following morning.

At the end of each day, I was exhausted. I couldn't wait to sleep, but I had no bed to sleep in. Yep, that's what I said. We slept on the floor on a very thin cushion with a thin pillow. I'm an American, and this was not easy for me, but I didn't complain. It made me greatly appreciate my life in America.

I shared a room with eleven other women who did not speak English. It was a hot summer, and all we had to cool us during the night was a fan. I often had non-fluent arguments with the Koreans about something called "fan death." There is a superstition that you can die in your sleep if you keep a fan on all night. Because of this belief, they would constantly get up to shut off the fan after I turned it on. I thought it was stupid, and whenever it got too hot to sleep, I would get up off the floor and turn it back on—only to have one of the women get up and turn it off. I yelled at her, but she continued to do it. This went on until one of us fell asleep. It was hot as hell. I was exhausted and beyond annoyed. With such little comfort, and that being the only small commodity to enjoy, I was pissed. I fought for it every night.

This room had one bathroom where the toilet and the open shower were next to each other, and we each took turns sharing them. The drain was often clogged by hair and other gross things, and we had to wear shoes while showering because the backed-up dirty bathwater almost covered our feet. It was really nasty, and it proved to be another challenge for me.

If I had ever imagined prison food, this was it. All meals were served in metal bowls. Breakfast consisted of a bowl of unseasoned plain white boiled rice and nothing else. Soy or duck sauce was nowhere to be found—and neither were salt or pepper or any condiments—and when I asked for them, they looked at me like I was a spoiled child. There was no chance of getting eggs, potatoes, cereal, bagels, or croissants—not even a cup of coffee. You ate what was being served—or you did not eat. That was it.

Lunch and dinner consisted of that same bowl of plain, unseasoned rice and some never-seen-before plant-scrub-grass-like side dishes that smelled and tasted bad. They occasionally served meat, but I didn't dare to try it. Remember mad cow disease? I'm now a vegetarian. Every day, you were guaranteed a side of kimchi, a well-known Korean side dish of pickled cabbage in hot cayenne pepper, which accompanied most meals. It was better in the States. In South Korea, it smelled rotten. For a week or so, I fought with bouts of explosive orange diarrhea—sorry for the graphics—and I was miserable.

I had brought some granola bars with me from the States, but I finished them within the first week because they turned out to be my daily meals instead of snacks.

Today, I ask for forgiveness for talking badly about such a great place. My words reflect my ungrateful mind at the time and not the kindness, generosity, and hospitality of that wonderful place. Shame on me for taking so long to see how ugly and ungrateful I truly was.

For a few hours on Saturday afternoons, we could leave the grounds and go sightseeing in the nearby areas. Happy to get a break from what felt like boot camp, a few of us decided to check out some shopping spots.

On one particular Saturday drive, we drove past a bunch of vendors selling different things on the sidewalk. One cage was full of beautiful small dogs that were jumping around. My face lit up in excitement, and I immediately asked our American driver to please stop so we could go play with them and pet them. For a moment, I *finally* felt happy about something.

The driver's eyes pierced at me through the rearview mirror, and he said, "You don't want to do that."

I didn't understand and asked, "Why not?"

He replied, "They are for sale as food."

I was shocked, saddened, and disgusted. I was so angry that I wanted to buy all of them and set them free, but I had nowhere to take them. My heart broke as we drove away because I hadn't been able to save them.

After my second week, I found a person with a phone who helped me call my father in America. When I finally got through, I must have sounded like I was calling from prison and needed him to rescue me. When I heard his voice, I immediately started speaking anxiously, "Dad! Hi, Dad! Dad, hi! Dad, it's me. I'm calling from Korea!"

He said, "Are you okay?"

I said yes, but I complained about the conditions, speaking a mile a minute the whole time.

He laughed and said, "I thought you were going there to find peace?"

Instead, I sounded like I had lost my mind.

I could not imagine tolerating another week there, but I didn't go all that way to quit. Even though I desperately longed to return to

America and all its blessings, I forced myself to stay. I felt like I was climbing the walls, and I wanted to rip out my hair. I had never felt the type of suffering where you weren't allowed to enjoy anything. It's interesting to see who you become when your comforts and pleasures are taken away. I didn't realize that this was a part of the healing process at the time. It brought out the true me and exposed me to the core.

Nothing about the trip was easy. Everything about it brought out the ugliest parts of me. I felt a lot of anger and resentment. I cursed and made rude facial expressions, and I regretted going. You would think under such conditions that this would be expected however, in actuality, they were signs of who I really was.

The day I was to return home was the first morning I had no problem waking up. On the plane, headed to freedom, I felt so immensely happy. I felt peace and tranquility in my soul. It was the first time I could watch TV in three weeks, and it seemed like such a luxury. I watched four movies and felt no discomfort in my tight plane seat on my thirteen-hour flight. I remembered feeling very uncomfortable and agitated on the way there. The meal on the plane tasted like it was made in a five-star restaurant. The passenger next to me was an overweight woman, and her elbow took ownership of my armrest during the entire flight, but it did not bother me. I wasn't even the slightest bit annoyed. In fact, I genuinely felt bad for her and leaned on the other armrest for most of the flight—just to give her more room.

I realized I was returning as a different person. I had been humbled. At last, it was clear that my miserable trip had benefitted me tremendously. I appreciated every little thing. It taught me *gratitude*! Gratitude is so powerful that it even changed a mule like me.

I thought about my constant complaints at the meditation center. I became ashamed at my behavior and pure lack of gratitude for whatever they were able to accommodate and offer me while I was there. I was able to clearly see how ungrateful I really was. We often think higher of ourselves than we truly are. May we each be stripped in such a way to value and appreciate all the brilliant gifts we already have and take for granted.

Gratitude adds so much to your life! It was another key element in my healing from depression.

The Importance of Meditation

Your true self is revealed through meditation. My eyes were like shutters that slowly opened as time passed. The more I meditated, the more they opened. The fog in my mind cleared. It was like a peek into my soul.

Before you start meditation, you will think that you're a much nicer person than you are, but after your true self is revealed, you will see what you're truly made of. You will clearly see the vanity, greed, evil, and other issues and insecurities that control and drive you. They will *never* bring you happiness or inner peace.

You might think you already know your strengths and weaknesses, but you don't. You must see it raw. An intense meditative state can reveal the traits you see as strength revealing themselves as weaknesses that are driven by uncovered issues.

I learned so much through meditation. Ego is an illusion to support self-esteem. Ego is prominent when we live in the make-believe images of our minds. It's all based on false thoughts; many were implanted early on and fed by societal beliefs. What we are led to believe as truth comes from the human mind, which is false, creating its only reality. Hence, you go after goals that come from the false mind and never achieve true happiness in your existence on earth. Meditation allows you to discern this.

Close your eyes for a minimum of two minutes in a quiet setting or when you go to bed tonight and pay attention to all the thoughts that swarm through your mind in that short amount of time. How can we truly enjoy life or gain inner peace with that mess in the way? Meditation clears the clutter.

In time, you will learn to kill these demons and begin to see what really matters, who you truly are, and the road to your actual life's purpose. My true self became revealed by clearing that clutter that ruled my mind for years.

As I meditated more, my mind grew clearer and clearer. It answered so many questions: Who am I? What is my purpose? What makes me truly happy? What changes must I make in my life to live happier and closer to my purpose?

The qualities and flaws of others will also become much more transparent to you. You will have little tolerance for certain individuals. You will naturally gravitate toward peaceful people and places. You will learn to live a simpler and happier life by appreciating more and needing less. It all happens naturally when you kill the pollution in your mind.

Through these revelations, I was able to see what changes I had to make in my life. In time, I executed them, which I will explain in the chapters to come.

Meditation has considerably changed me. Before meditation, I used to talk much louder, be super obnoxious, and be much more impatient than I am now. Things that once made me angry now make me cry. I am more selfless in nature. I have more compassion, empathy, and sympathy for others. I live with so much more inner peace and love.

I have learned that if you don't connect with yourself on a spiritual level to cure *you*, you will never cure yourself from the outside world. It does not matter who you are or what you have. Everything is temporary. Only your soul is forever. Fill it with peace.

For me, meditation has proven to be extremely beneficial for mental health and for my entire life. I am eternally grateful.

Chapter 13
Volunteering and Giving Back

There are many different kinds of people in the world. Many spend their whole lives trying to gain some sort of power, status, and/or fame, but when you look at one of the most influential beings who ever lived, Mother Teresa, she sought only to give of herself to benefit others.

Mother Teresa lived among the poor, using her greatest possession—her instrument of love—to make an incredible impact on the world. Mother Teresa was a true example of love being the most powerful element in the world. With her acts of love, she touched thousands. She was so powerful that even after her death, her selfless acts continue to influence people all over the globe, including me. Seeing someone's soul is a beautiful thing.

They say that you are attracted to certain individuals in life because you admire them—and because you might also subconsciously want to be like them. I didn't realize this at first when I found myself drawn to Mother Teresa. However, after meditation, it was revealed to me why I had felt such a strong connection to her for several years. What I love in her is what lives in me: the desire to help the poor and less fortunate with special sensitivity to children. It hurts me deeply to see these innocent angels coming into the world, at the beginning of life, and instead of feeling the joy and magic of childhood, they are abandoned, abused, hungry, and/or ill. I wanted to help somehow, and I took the first step to do so.

Becoming a Doula

Still in my depressive state, I felt the urge to take a step forward and do something. I went to the local children's hospital and decided to become a doula for terminally ill children.

A question on the application asked why I wanted to volunteer with sick children. I answered honestly and said, "God sent me here." For a second, I wondered if I would be ridiculed for my answer, but then realized I did not care about people who would think that way.

I didn't think I was in any condition to be able to help others since I still needed help myself, but I kept feeling the call within. I didn't know if I would be strong enough to face these ill children, but I knew something bigger than me knew I could. I didn't know what to expect, and the thought of getting attached to a child and then having them die scared me. I didn't have children of my own and couldn't imagine the pain of such a loss. I also didn't think I could endure any more pain, but I was strongly drawn to this purpose. I was determined to focus on the love and comfort I could provide instead of my own selfish fears.

I had never done anything like it before. It was entirely an altruistic act. I was very surprised to find out that the benefits of volunteering included an amazing reciprocation for my own healing, soul growth, and spiritual development.

On my first day at the children's hospital, I parked in the lot and sat in my car, looked up at the sky, and said, "God, you sent me here. You must think I am strong enough to do this—so here I go." I felt anxious and nervous. I was afraid of catching something, but I gathered what little energy I had and went inside because I strongly believed it was my mission.

I envisioned spending time with children, playing with them, singing to them, reading to them, and making them laugh to help brighten up their spirits. I expected the children, although battling illness, would still be able to physically interact with me and be playful. However, the child I was assigned to was nothing like I imagined.

This one-year-old girl had been born with brain damage and physical deformities. She was kept alive by a ventilator and a feeding tube. She was completely unresponsive and blind. Her eyes were taped shut, and the doctors also believed she was deaf. Her legs were turned outward and didn't bend; the right one stiffly pointed straight out of the right side of her body. She was only kept alive by the machines. It was an extremely sad sight, and I wondered how I would possibly be able to help this child. I had no idea how this situation could help my own depressive state.

When I first saw her, I was flushed with so many different emotions running through me. I held back my tears and felt like I was choking. I was frozen as I looking at her. I felt helpless—and like a failure in my quest to do good. I thought, *What can I possibly do to help her? This is only going to make me sadder.*

It was my first day, and I did not want to be a failure or to fail without even trying. My mind was flooded with so many thoughts and questions:

- Why are they keeping her alive? It seemed pointless, almost cruel. She couldn't do anything but lie there.
- Can she even hear or feel when the nurses touch her?
- Where are her parents?
- Do I still want to have children?
- What is God trying to teach me?

Looking back, I was immediately taught, in that very moment, to appreciate what I already had in my life while so many have it so much worse. Sufferers of depression know that seeing it is not enough to provide a cure. However, it is a path toward it.

At first, I didn't know what to do during my visits. I felt sad when I even looked at her. I don't really know why, but I was afraid to touch her at first. I didn't know if she could even feel me. It was such unfamiliar territory for me.

Since I didn't know how to handle her or what to do, I just did what my heart told me and started reading *My Daily Bread*. I didn't even know if she could hear me. As I read, I began to wonder if I was reading for her or for me—or for both of us.

As the weeks went by, she seemed to be doing better. I didn't understand how that could be because she remained in the same critical condition, but in my eyes, she seemed to look better. I still didn't talk to her for several weeks. It felt weird to talk to her. *Can she even hear me?* I continued to read to her and hoped the prayers would soothe her soul. They definitely soothed mine.

As the months went by, I became closer to her. I even started missing her if a few days went by without seeing her. I tried to visit at least three times per week.

Slowly, I began to touch her by softly caressing and then eventually massaging her limbs, hands, chest, face, and scalp. I even started to wipe the drool that often flowed down her cheek when she needed to be suctioned or was too warm. I also found that she was ticklish when I caressed her upper chest near her right armpit; she kicked up her right foot and turned red. I was learning about her. In time, I slowly began to speak to her. It now seemed senseless not to. I always greeted her, reminded her of my name, and told her that I was her friend visiting her. I also told her that I missed her.

After a few weeks, I noticed she was making sounds. It felt like she was trying to communicate with me and knew who I was. I became more familiar with her and the way she responded—even though it was very subtle and hard to recognize at first. I don't believe she was completely deaf. I sensed that she loved music. I often sang to her and played nursery rhymes for her to listen to when I left. I could clearly see that she was better after my visits. When I arrived, her body was usually cold and stiff, but by the time I left, her cheeks were flushed and her body was warmer. I was happy that my visits were comforting her.

Many times, I would look at her and question God's purpose for her. Only He knows what He is doing. We are only a grain of sand in His whole picture. When I met her, I questioned why they were keeping her alive, but I came to the point where I thought God had left her in that condition for a reason.

On one of my visits, I was in awe at a thought that came to mind. I realized that her condition might be her life's purpose! *She is an example of all the blessings that we have and take for granted. It's true because every time I see her, I appreciate my own health and the many blessings I have. Think about it. She is a teacher and a healer! She teaches gratitude. Wow! Now, that's powerful! Every single life does have a purpose.*

I thought about her condition. *She can't see, move, possibly hear, eat, drink, talk, play, or even smile. I can do all those things, but I am depressed.* I felt ashamed. I felt so ungrateful for all that I was and all that I had. That was another part of my healing. Gratitude truly heals the world.

I came to the point where, after each visit, I would thank her immensely for what she had taught me. I realized that she had given me so much more than I had given her—even in her condition. What a profound experience!

To think that I once questioned why they were keeping her alive in such a condition.

Thank you, God, for gained wisdom and another lesson learned. And thank you, God's little angel on earth.

***

Within a year or so of becoming a doula in the children's hospital, I also started volunteering at nonprofit residential treatment facility and school for troubled children. I joined a classroom full of young boys who were abandoned, abused, and/or deprived situations. I felt honored to work with them and give them the time, attention, and respect they weren't used to being given. They responded so well to it, which was no surprise since love is a natural healer.

Self-Reflection

The true self is built on selflessness. I am so grateful that I no longer live just for the person reflected in the mirror. Our wealth is within us—and so is the ability to change the world. I now clearly see that I have spent most of my life living for earthly possessions and personal benefit instead of helping others or contributing to a better world. Of course, that will only result in feeling empty, depressed, and alone. No good comes from selfishness and greed.

My life has so much more meaning now. I am giving more and needing less. It is a life filled with giving and receiving love. It is very much worth living.

When you come to the point in your life when you realize there is nothing you truly need that money can buy, you have come pretty close to mastering your life.

My focus now is on more positive worldly issues, symbols of peace, good deeds, awareness, and ideas to better ourselves and our world through an abundance of love and light. We all need to start to follow a new world awareness trend and give less energy and time to things that only benefit ourselves.

Most recently, I have extended humanitarian acts to world hunger issues. Specifically, I wanted to find out why food in large institutions such as hospitals was being discarded every night instead of being distributed to local shelters. I learned about the Bill Emerson Good Samaritan Act of 1996 and met with the person in charge of the hospital cafeteria where I worked. Now, I am working to have all the food that used to be discarded to instead be distributed to feed hundreds of people at nearby shelters. I felt great to be able to help others in that way. It is not hard to make a difference. Anyone can do it!

As I researched ways to increase aid from other large institutions, I became aware of the direct effects of eating meat on world hunger. Apparently, we have enough grain to feed the entire world, but it is being used to feed animals that are slaughtered for the profit of their meat. People starve to death—and animals get killed for profit? Double negative. This is inhumane and extremely disturbing.

I immediately became a vegetarian to become a part of a solution and to stop contributing to the problem. Vegans deserve much respect. Although many of us need to take baby steps with our diet changes, we can all make a difference. Even Albert Einstein, one of the world's greatest minds, knew it when he said, "Nothing will benefit human health and increase chances of survival of life on earth as much as the evolution to a vegetarian diet."

Chapter 14

The Metamorphosis of Me—My Awakening

For a large part of my life, I was very skeptical about things I could not see or explain, including God—until the passing of my brother. However, in time, I have grown spiritually through many extraordinary experiences. I learned that, besides God, there are angels, spirit guides, deceased loved ones, and other loving things among us.

A few days after the loss of my brother, I started noticing strange, unexplainable occurrences. He was communicating with me and other family members through electricity. It started when my phone rang in a very unusual (British-type) manner, at exactly 10:31 p.m., which was the house address where we grew up together.

That same week, his wife told me that she was watching television in bed with their two young children, and the channel suddenly changed itself to one of his favorite shows.

Later that week, someone rang my sister's doorbell, but when she opened it, no one was there. The distance from her door to the street was not so close that someone would have time to ring it and run. I believe he was reaching out to let us know that he was okay and that he still exists in some form. It was fascinating and comforting.

He still visits me often through my dreams, almost two

decades later. This isn't an opinion. He does. Some will try to say I subconsciously manifest this, but it is not so. He just pops up randomly—even if the dream doesn't have anything to do with him. He is a quiet visitor. I love it. A warm sense of love overwhelms me when he shows up. No one else makes me feel that way. It's our special bond and connection. I feel like he is telling me that I am not alone. It's so nice to still have him—even if only in my dreams.

In one particularly unusual dream, I was struggling with a conflict that I was having with my family in real life. In my dream, I was in a bed, and out of nowhere, he appeared next to me and spread mayonnaise on my arm. Strange, huh? I was not very annoyed with him in the dream because he was known to joke around like that. He wasn't smiling or showing any other facial expressions, but he usually doesn't when he visits my dreams. He communicates through feelings, usually of warmth and love. Some people have said their loved ones communicate verbally in their dreams, but this has not been my experience.

When I woke up from that dream, I reflected at how unusual and random it was. I wondered if it was a message, and I looked up mayonnaise in my Dream Dictionary App. It pertained to the exact situation I was going through with my family! I was dumbfounded. He was letting me know that he was there with me through it all. I was not alone. It gave me such comfort and feelings of love and support. He never turned his back on me—not even in the afterlife. *That* is true unconditional love.

To make sense of the paranormal, we must turn away from the logical and go toward the metaphysical. These are things you cannot explain, yet they can't be denied—whether you wish to accept them or not. I am more than grateful to have had these experiences and accept them as proof that the soul *does* go on. This also brings peace, acceptance, and hope.

I completely believe that we are spiritual beings in physical bodies and not physical beings having spiritual experiences. Through years of personal experiences and intense meditations, I have confirmed this belief. I also believe that ascension happens during life and not after death—and it may take many lives to completely ascend.

Angelic Messages

A different kind of experience occurred at a Barnes & Noble about a decade ago. I was in the New Age section (a favorite at the time), and a misfiled book fell off of the shelf. It was *Sacred Signs* by Adrian Calabrese. I was completely clueless about spirituality at the time, but I skimmed through it and felt compelled to research it further. I purchased it. It was time to evolve.

The book was leading me down my spiritual path. That essential piece had been missing in my life; it was a necessary part of my growth. It was no coincidence, especially since I don't believe in coincidences. The book was meant to fall into my hands. God—or whatever you believe in—is constantly sending us signs to help us. We just need to be present and aware of them. If you read the book, you will understand.

After reading it and opening myself to that world, I started receiving many more messages from the spiritual world. Maybe I was just becoming more aware of them. A few weeks later, in that same aisle, a customer mentioned that he liked the angel wings on my shirt, which I hadn't even noticed. He told me it was a sign for him since he had asked for one from his angels. *A sign?* I was so in awe of such things at the time. *A spiritual world outside of religion?* This new world intrigued me.

I had been struggling with completely believing in God or angels, but it felt like something was trying to help me believe. It was as if we were sent to deliver messages to each other from above. I was eager to learn more and asked this young man some questions about his belief in angels. He introduced me to *The Lightworker's Source* by Sahvanna Arienta.

It quickly become my favorite book since it described exactly who I felt I was becoming or already was all along. I always felt misunderstood—even by myself. I never knew why I was driven to say or feel the things that I did. Why was I so different than most? People often said, "You're different" or "You're special."

That beautiful book completely filled my heart with love. I was convinced that angels had contacted me and helped me along my path. I also discovered that I am a lightworker: a unique soul that incarnated here for a special purpose. It made so much sense and was very liberating to discover.

Many of the things I have felt and desired finally made sense. I love much deeper than most, and I suffer much deeper too. I cry very easily and absorb other people's emotions, especially those who are suffering. This includes complete strangers. I instantly cry when I see other people crying. It can be quite overwhelming and emotionally draining. I am trying to learn to observe without absorbing. As A. P. Gouthey said, "He helps others most, who shows them how to help themselves."

After learning about lightworkers, I researched angels for four or five months. Within a few weeks, I began receiving signs of their presence. If someone had told me that a few years ago, I would've thought they were nuts, but it was proven to me. It was a beautiful and magical experience.

The First Signs

I had never had a cricket inside my home in New York City in the years I lived there. I had never even heard one in the neighborhood. Heck, I hadn't even seen one since I was a child. One day, I saw one inside my home. Although I was surprised, I didn't think too much about it. I never intentionally kill insects so I swept it in a dustpan and set it free out the front door. A couple of days later, another one arrived.

Later that evening, I was meditating in the shower and thought about how bizarre it was to see two crickets in my home within a week since I had never seen a single one in the years I lived there.

I wondered if it was a sign. I later googled the spiritual meaning of crickets, and sure enough, it was a sign! *Wow,* I thought. *It is fascinating. How do they physically manifest like that? I guess when you believe in God, you're not supposed to doubt anything.*

For months after that, I started to notice series of numbers in the hour of the day, addresses, bills, or other sequences with the numbers 1111,111, which also has a spiritual meaning. It was almost daily, and it was always unexpected. There was so much divine intervention trying to help me through my depression that it would be foolish to ignore or not believe. I started to feel alive. I knew there was more helping and protecting us than what we can see. I felt so loved and special!

My personally-requested spiritual sign was a ladybug. I would often see them in the most unexpected areas, confirming that I was on the right path. Recently, I started finding dimes and even a ten-dollar bill while I was awaiting acceptance from publishers for this book. It was validation that I was on the right path.

Angelic Intervention at the Roulette Table

A friend from work invited me to join her and another friend on a trip to Atlantic City. Being a loner at times, I separated from them and took a walk by myself. Just for kicks, I decided to join in for a single spin at the roulette table. I put all my chips on the number eleven since it had angelic significance to me. No matter if I won or lost, I felt content and peaceful with my decision.

Well, the number eleven hit! What were the chances? I smiled from ear to ear, kindly collected my winnings, bid the other players a lovely day, and walked away. They all looked at this swift ordeal and at me as if saying, "What the hell was that? Who was that girl?"

It was rather amusing, but it was even more magical. Many people would just say it was mere luck, but I know it was more than that. It was angelic intervention. It was beautiful.

I started feeling hope restored within; it was another necessary step toward healing from my depression.

The Psychic Connection

During this awakening phase, I went to see a psychic with a friend, never expecting anything from it but entertainment.

For several years, I had been contemplating whether I should publish this book. Although I had been writing it for years, I didn't initially intend to have it published. I couldn't imagine sharing such private experiences or putting my mistakes on blast and then having to deal with ignorant and undesirable comments or judgments. I initially wrote only for a therapeutic release until I realized it was essential to share, in the efforts to help heal others. Self-sacrifice was imperative.

When I sat with the psychic and gave her my palm, the first thing she said was, "Why aren't you writing?"

I immediately froze and looked at her like she had three heads. I had never met her before.

She said, "Don't doubt it."

I felt like I was floating above my chair when I heard that. She could've said a million different things; instead, she hit exactly on my greatest concern.

Today, I have learned that the Bible—and probably other religious teachings—are against psychics, but I believed that angels sent that message to me through her. I was so happy and felt such a sense of purpose. I finally felt 100 percent that, no matter what obstacles I feared, by releasing this book, I was being given the confidence, encouragement, and support to do it. That's when I finally decided to write my book without fear because that was what I was supposed to do.

I had never felt so sure about anything before. It was a life-changing moment. Suddenly, the world felt like such a magical place filled with love, hope, and support. I hadn't felt these feelings during any of the years I suffered from depression. As I became spiritually awakened, I was slowly coming back to life.

Imagine what it felt like when not too long before this, I no longer wanted to live.

Some readers may attempt to label this new belief as a desperate attempt to self-medicate from depression, but these were true experiences that were not created in the mind. During my depression, I wanted to die—not medicate myself. So, you must believe in the supernatural because it is proven to be real.

I was given such a hopeful revelation that I was *not* alone through my struggles. I knew God and His angels were guiding me to fulfill my life's purpose. It gave me something to look forward to, and it felt good to know I had a reason to live. I realized my struggles and pain were meant to heal others—and possibly save someone's life!

For the first time in years, I cried tears of joy.

Escape to Spain

In 2015, I planned a trip and traveled to Spain for a month of introspection. I decided to spend it on the island of Ibiza, far away from my life in New York City, to solely focus on re-centering myself and writing this book. Ibiza is known for partying, but I did no drinking, partying, or any other craziness that I had heard went on there. I was a writer on a mission.

I ended up connecting most with the hippies in Ibiza, many of whom lived in the forest, as one with nature. They were very peaceful, happy, simple, and free. Many were talented artists who would play drums, guitars, and other instruments and sing on the beach as tourists crowded around them. I couldn't stop smiling around them. I hadn't smiled like that in years. Their energy was so light. Inside, I felt like I was one of them—or needed to be.

It was very beneficial to see how other people around the world lived. They didn't even appear to have anything to deal with because they just existed in the moment and not in their minds. It taught me a lot. I became very aware of how different I was from them. I really noticed my flaws.

I realized that at some point during my downfall, I had started taking life way too seriously. I obsessively worried about things that hadn't even happened yet—and might never happen. I couldn't imagine just letting things fall into place. I needed to have control of everything, and when I couldn't, I lost myself. It was an inevitable setup for failure and disappointment.

How many times do we make plans in life that never turn out as planned? That's why people say, "You plan—and God laughs."

I was overthinking every single issue and making mountains out of molehills. That brought an overload of anxiety and negativity, which made overcoming depression that much harder.

In your life, job, or relationship, you should not feel like you are constantly climbing rocks. It is a sign that you're going against the natural flow of the current. I needed to relax and just let life happen.

I wrote this revelation while I was there:

The cluttered mind lives in fear, worry, and tomorrow.
The peaceful, happy mind lives in the *now*.
So be present and enjoy this moment.
Don't lose it to the worries of tomorrow and the unknown.

Overthinking is mental noise. It is a distraction from peace, clarity, the true answers, and your present moment. The way you direct your mind by controlling your thoughts is how you live your life—either positively or negatively. I am working on mastering this more and more each day, and I am learning to live by the laws of attraction. Your mind can become your deadliest enemy. It's not an easy process to retrain your mind, but it is a necessary one.

We must figure out who we are and not what society, our parents, or anything else has instilled in us. Be who you are—no matter how different it is from others. Be original and unafraid of expression. Just be you and be present.

B-U

You don't need to fit in.
You need to be true.
Be who you are.
Just *be you.*

Act how you feel—
Not how is expected.
Judged by sinners,
Don't fear rejection.

Don't need to follow.
Lead and be free.
Free of expression.
Free to *just be.*

Love who you are.
Hold your head up high.
You are your own star.
Express your self-pride.

Do what's right.
Don't follow the wrong.
Live in the light.
Stay out of the fog.

Don't be shallow.
Look deep within.
Love yourself and others.
You'll always win.

Ayahuasca in Brazil

Later that year, after much research on the vine known as ayahuasca, which I heard about in Ibiza, I decided I wanted to expand my research and try it. I went on a nine-day retreat to the middle of the jungle in Itacaré, Brazil. I was on a mission of healing and discovery. The amazing Amazonian practice was an extraordinary experience.

This particular retreat is owned and managed by a licensed clinical psychologist, Silvia Polivoy, who gave up her profession to solely work with the plant and start the Spirit Vine Retreat. I felt very safe under her supervision. It was located in the middle of the jungle in a beautiful, serene, peaceful place; it was the perfect setting for such an experience.

Ayahuasca is not a drug. It comes from a tropical vine that is native to the Amazon region, and it is known for its hallucinogenic properties. A drink that is made from the bark of this vine has been used for centuries in the Amazon. It brings heightened awareness of the inner self with no addictive properties. It is not habitual, but it is desired.

I have never had a "tripping" experience. I will say that it is an experience, to date, that exceeds anything I have ever undertaken or imagined existed. It was a unique and supernatural experience. This experience is hard to explain in words since it is truly magical, but I will do my best to try to describe it for you. You should know that words do not give it justice.

The retreat was organized effectively. All the attendees are joined in a round bungalow of sorts, in the jungle, and seated in a circle with other people who have also traveled from around the world for the experience. You have your ayahuasca tea, the lights go off, shamanic music goes on, and you can either sit on the floor or lie down and wait for the tea to kick in, which is pretty quick, and the visions begin. The tea is a distasteful, thick, dark liquid that is served with a piece of lime.

For several hours, you have revelations and messages from a

higher being, somewhere deep within your subconscious or from an unknown messenger. The messages are very clear, and you will see visions of past and present in such sharp resolution and never-before-seen psychedelic designs of flowing patterns and colors in motion. All the while, you are fully awake with your eyes closed. Your visions can be dark and depressing or peaceful and blissful; it all depends on what lives in you and what surfaces from your subconscious.

I felt deep interior pain and suffering, and at other times, I felt pure heavenly bliss that I had never felt in real life.

You will receive messages and unveiling of things about yourself, such as habits, fears, and many, many more different areas of your life. It takes you to dimensions you have never been to—dimensions that you did not know existed. You cannot even imagine them. It will be the closest to God or a higher power you have ever been. Any skeptics should experience it *first* in order to give an intelligent opinion about it. This experience is beyond your wildest dreams!

I received several messages that made clear sense to me. For example, when I fell into depression, I forgot how to have fun and just be present. I received a message urging me to get back into dance classes, which I had completely stopped due to my depressive state.

I also was shown why I dated the wrong men. Subconsciously, I only dated men I thought my father would approve of—being from my own culture. Of course, the relationships would not work because they were coming from a desire of condition.

Before the ceremony, you can ask a question projected to Mother Ayahuasca (as it is called) for her to show you an answer. During one of these ceremonies, I asked how I could heal others if I'm not healed myself. I struggled with this concern because I genuinely believed my mission was to help others heal, but I felt inadequate to do so without being completely healed myself first.

After drinking the tea, the answer I received was profound. It came from a powerful feminine energy. A higher being spoke to me and clearly told me that I can heal others through my own healing. It made complete sense. It gave me the reassurance that I needed to continue pursuing this. It was another confirmation that this book must be published.

I also experienced very frequent urges to yawn. I constantly yawned uncontrollably between visions for what felt like hours. This was linked to the past few years when I had become overanalytical, literal, uptight, and tense. This message was telling me to loosen up, breathe, and relax!

Another significant message came after days of my body purging, thrusting, and softly moaning during the ceremony. It was as if I was being sexually pleased. I was embarrassed but couldn't stop the way that I felt. In fact, I was unaware that it went on for hours. I was told later by the guy next to me—a hottie—and I couldn't look at him after that.

I couldn't understand this message at first, but when it happened again at the next ceremony, I was shown the answer. The purging and thrusting were showing me that I had to let go and release all pent-up attachments, feelings of the past, and whatever else was holding me back from moving forward. The message was on point.

The whole experience is subjective since each individual has their own visions and messages. I have not met anyone who didn't agree with how amazing the experience is. I highly recommend it to the right candidates; google the requirements to see if it's for you. For example, you cannot be on any stimulants, antidepressants, and certain other meds several days prior to a ceremony.

I cannot give ayahuasca the merit it deserves in words. There are not enough words in the English language to describe it, and the word "amazing" doesn't even come close. It is above you. Trust me. It is above us all.

Where Is Home?

Some people say, "Home is where the heart is." Those words, however, never resonated within me as anything other than sweet words.

On my many flights to visit family or on vacations, I often

found myself looking out of the window and feeling overwhelmed by the empty and lost feeling of not belonging. I've always felt like a phantom through life. I felt like a lost soul.

- Where is home?
- Why have I not found a place where I can feel like I'm truly at home?
- Is there a void within me that needs to be filled in order to finally feel it?
- Most importantly, how can I find home when I don't even know where or what it is?

After my spiritual awakening, I started to feel it as I evolved and got closer to God by reading *My Daily Bread*. I have come to learn that home is inner peace, and since I hadn't felt that within, I could never feel it anywhere outside of myself.

In conclusion, home is in the heart of a person who has inner peace.

Chapter 15
Recycling My Life

From Break to Hope and from Pain to Peace

With a newfound outlook on life and my life's purpose, I realized I needed to live what I hungered for the most: inner peace. To do this, I knew that I had to make swift and drastic changes to my life. I decided that I was going to eliminate anything that didn't bring or add light into my life.

I evaluated all aspects of my life, including my job, the places I hung out, my friends, and even my relatives. I quickly began to remove any negative people, places, influences, and other distractions that did not merit time or space in my mind or life. I wanted only positivity.

Insincere people, gossipers, and those who were fake, jealous, or did not genuinely care about me had to be eliminated completely. I could no longer tolerate the cesspool of ignorance or continue to waste my precious time and energy on it. It was very easy to weed those people out my life. *Why did I ever think I needed them or even associate with such toxic individuals in the first place? Good riddance.*

I would rather have one loyal, loving, true friend than twenty of those.

This reminds me of a self-reflective quote by Jim Rohn that I appreciate: "You are the average of the five people you spend the most time with." It reminded me that I need to surround myself with like-minded, intelligent, peaceful, and loving individuals who also want to make the world a better place. Anything less would be a setback to my dreams and goals- and to the peace of my existence.

Things that I promptly recycled or changed:

- I removed negative people and places.
- I joined a gym and ate healthier.
- I painted and did more writing.
- I started taking guitar lessons and dance classes.
- I went for walks in nature to ground myself.
- I had more time to volunteer.
- I was less distracted in my daily meditations.
- I joined an online dating site to open up my heart to love.
- I focused on being grateful every day.
- I disconnected from my social media accounts.

When I was done with these changes, which was a transition that only took a few months, my life almost instantly started to simplify. I became so much more peaceful. I had fewer distractions and a clearer mind. It created a vacuum of space that I could fill with things that benefitted my soul and the world.

I was pleased to finally see that I was clearly healing and evolving. I thought differently, behaved differently, felt calmer and more peaceful, and changed my belief system. I was more worldly and less self-centered. I became acutely aware of the importance and power I possess in my life.

Through meditation (clearing of the mind), recycling my life (cleaning up my life), and volunteering (becoming selfless and grateful), my true self was finally exposed. My walls were all breaking down and exposing me. I was more naked and visible than I'd ever felt or been. I was so humbled. Most importantly, I was given a new breath of life.

These positive changes were fundamental to my healing from

the darkness of depression, which had owned me for so long. I was at a turning point in my life. It was a rebirth.

***

I have been connecting with God more and more these days. In *My Daily Bread*, Anthony J. Paone, SJ, said, "I will find reason to praise him even when life seems dark and unbearable." If you follow God through it all, you will never be alone.

This reminds me of a ninety-five-year-old woman I recently met. During a brief conversation, I asked if she could give me some words of wisdom for living a good life.

Without hesitation, she replied, "Believe in God."

Chapter 16
Finding the Light

The person in the first few chapters of this book is unknown to me today; she is a stranger in the baby steps of individual growth. I have been completely reinvented and continually evolving. There is much more to come, and I am excited about this new journey of light expansion.

Like many, I have fallen off the wagon many times. I am not special. We all have suffered, but the point is to keep getting back up, and no matter how much it hurts, believe that that pain is leading you to something greater. That greatness will diminish your suffering and lead to a much greater version of yourself. Each time you get back up, you are not the person you were prior to that experience. You are wiser and more gifted.

What I have ultimately learned through life's struggles is that the only way to fully live a life is to live it for others. Imagine the profound impact it would have on the world if we each did something—no matter how small.

We are all works in progress, but when we go against our life's purpose (our true self), we will hit a lot of friction, stress, and turmoil, which can lead to depression or even suicide, depending on the magnitude of our divergence. We must accept when something is just not meant to be. You can never swim upstream when the flow is naturally downstream and effortless. Trust your feelings. Trust your mind and heart—not just your heart.

Your life's purpose is to live your bliss. The road to your bliss is filled with love and not resistance. Depression does not reside there.

Without my suffering, this book would never have made it into your hands. It is now clear that I have had to have parts of me die in order to live. I now see beauty where I once thought it did not exist. I possess a soul with so much depth. It is rich in compassion and contains more selfless love than I have ever known. This unveiling brings a larger purpose than I ever imagined: the ability to heal others.

I see myself taking this further and using these gifts to continue this journey. This book is only the first step.

I am hopeful that this book provides light and hope to others who are suffering from depression or who feel lost in their lives. I hope they have learned through my story, as well as their own, that sometimes we need to be peeled like an onion, crying our way from one disappointment to another, before we are able to reveal the diamond in the center of our souls. Don't doubt it. It's there.

Nothing is over until the moment you stop trying. Do not give up. The obstacle is the path. Know that, even in your darkest hour, the light will shine again. May you each find and radiate that light within to heal yourself and extend it to the world.♥

Printed in the United States
By Bookmasters